513 WEIRD FACTS

THAT EVERY KID SHOULD KNOW

ARCTURUS

This edition published in 2022 by Arcturus Publishing Limited
26/27 Bickels Yard, 151–153 Bermondsey Street,
London SE1 3HA

Illustrator: Luke Séguin-Magee
Authors: Thomas Canavan, Marc Powell, Anne Rooney, and William Potter
Designer and Editor: Lucy Doncaster
Design Manager: Jessica Holliland
Managing Editor: Joe Harris

ISBN: 978-1-3988-2761-5
CH011209NT
Supplier 26, Date 1222, PI 00003003

Printed in China

CONTENTS

 INTRODUCTION

Are you fascinated by the weird and wonderful world of science, space, the human body, and all things furry, feathery, fanged, and fierce? Yes?! Then prepare to be astounded, intrigued, or totally grossed out by the hundreds of fabulous facts that follow.

Divided into four sections, this book takes a look at all sorts of incredible facts. To start with, learn more about how our world works—from why people on the other side of the world don't fall off to what causes ocean waves, and whether you can bang in a nail with a banana.

Staying in the natural world, it's time to meet the beasts! Delve into the wild and wacky kingdom of animals and discover how much poop a black rhino produces every day, how to hypnotize a chicken, and which creature loves stinky feet.

Humans are up next, in all their gory glory. Learn more about our brains, bones, muscles, heart, and much more. Find out why your tummy rumbles when you're hungry, how fast air moves when you sneeze, and whether you can taste with your nose.

Finally, it's time to blast off into a whole universe of mindblowing wonders as you explore the far reaches of the Universe. From space spiders and moon landings to black holes and aliens, prepare to be astounded by all things intergalactic—the facts are out of this world!

So, are you ready? Then ...

5 ...
4 ...
3 ...
2 ...
1 ...

LET'S GO!

STRANGE SCIENCE

WHY IS MOST OF THE WORLD'S LAND NORTH OF THE EQUATOR?

It just happens to be that way at the moment. Believe it or not, the Earth's continents are slowly moving. Around 300 million years ago, our planet had one big mass of land called Pangaea. It was mainly south of the equator. In another 200 million years, things will probably look different again.

HOW MUCH OF THE EARTH IS COVERED BY ICE?

Just under 10 percent of Earth is covered by ice. Most of that ice is in the glaciers and ice caps of Greenland and Antarctica. Snow and ice also cover mountains in other parts of the world all year long.

WHY DOES IT GET HOTTER IN THE SUMMER?

During summer, the northern hemisphere (the Earth's top half) is tilted toward the Sun. It gets more sunlight and becomes hotter. At this time, the southern hemisphere has winter. Then things swap six months later when the bottom half is closer to the Sun.

HOW FAR AWAY IS THE HORIZON?

It depends on your height! The taller or higher up you are, the greater the distance you'll be able to see before the curve of the Earth dips out of sight. For a girl who is 1.4 m (4 foot 7 inches) tall, the horizon would be 4.2 km (2.6 miles) away. But if she stood on a 3 m (10 foot) ladder, the horizon would be 7.5 km (4.6 miles) away.

DOES EVERY THUNDERSTORM HAVE LIGHTNING?

The answer is very simple—yes. Lightning causes thunder. A lightning bolt quickly heats up air. The hot air expands and then quickly cools and contracts. That super-fast heating and cooling makes the sound of thunder.

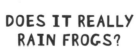

DOES IT REALLY RAIN FROGS?

Yes, but not very often. A very powerful storm can suck frogs and fish up from rivers, lakes, and the sea. They are held up by strong, spinning winds. Then they fall back down when the winds weaken.

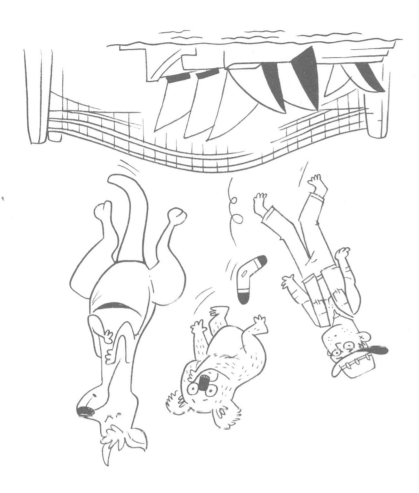

WHY DON'T PEOPLE IN THE SOUTHERN HEMISPHERE FALL OFF THE EARTH?

People in the southern hemisphere are not upside down. It's just that most maps are drawn with the southern hemisphere at the bottom. An upside down map would be just as accurate. In fact, gravity pulls everything into the core of the Earth, so we all stay on it!

IS THE EARTH SLOWING DOWN?

Yes, it is. The exact length of a day (one complete spin of the planet) on Earth is 23 hours and 56 minutes. However, the Earth is slowing down by about one second every ten years. So in 2,400 years, a day really will last exactly 24 hours.

IS THE EARTH COMPLETELY ROUND?

Not quite! Its spinning makes the Earth a little wider along the equator and shorter at the poles. The distance through the Earth from North Pole to South Pole is less than the distance through the Earth at the equator.

WHY DOES THE MOON SEEM SO BIG WHEN IT'S JUST RISING OVER THE HORIZON?

Scientists know that it's a trick that our eyes play on us. However, they can't agree on how it works. To show that the Moon doesn't change size, hold a coin out so it just covers the Moon on the horizon. Hold it at the same distance when the Moon is overhead. You won't see any change in size.

WHAT IS AN ECHO?

An echo is simply a reflection of sound just as a mirror image is a reflection of light. Sound travels in waves. When these waves hit a hard surface, they bounce back. We hear the sound again a little later (once it has gone to the hard surface and back).

DO YOU REALLY HEAR THE OCEAN IF YOU PUT A SEASHELL TO YOUR EAR?

What you hear are the sounds around you—background noise. These sounds are bouncing around inside the shell. You hear those bounced-around sounds as a "whoosh," and your brain decides it's the sound of the ocean. Why? Probably because you're holding a seashell.

CAN ANIMALS PREDICT EARTHQUAKES?

The answer seems to be "yes" for some animals. Frogs and toads can sense slight chemical changes in the water in ponds or lakes. Scientists have noticed similar changes in rocks in the days leading up to earthquakes. Witnesses have seen groups of toads leaving ponds just before earthquakes.

WHY DO VOLCANOES ERUPT?

The Earth's crust (outer layer) is made up of large pieces called plates. Magma, a gooey substance made up of gas and melted rock, lies under the plates. When two plates collide, they may force magma to the surface in a volcanic eruption. The magma that comes out is called lava.

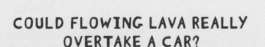

COULD FLOWING LAVA REALLY OVERTAKE A CAR?

The speed of a lava flow differs from volcano to volcano. A lot depends on how steep the slope is. The amount of gas mixed in with the molten (melted) rock also affects how "runny" the lava is. Witnesses have recorded lava flowing faster than 60 km/h (38 mph) —fast enough to overtake a car.

CAN PLANTS TURN TO STONE?

The word petrified means "turned to stone." This can happen to plants or animals after they have died. Water that has minerals in it dissolves the plant's soft tissue. The harder parts, such as the tubes and bark, don't dissolve. The minerals take less than 100 years to harden. By then, the plant still looks like a plant, but it is now made of stone.

WHY ARE BEACHES SANDY?

Sand is simply rock that has been broken into very small pieces. These pieces are less than 2 mm (0.08 in) across. Every beach was once made of solid rock. The sea's pounding waves grind coastal rocks into small pieces over thousands of years.

DID A METEORITE REALLY KILL OFF THE DINOSAURS?

Dinosaurs were common across the world for many millions of years. Then all signs of them stopped about 65 million years ago. Their disappearance was a mystery for many years. Most scientists now agree that a large meteorite (a stone from space that crashes to Earth) hit our planet about 65 million years ago. It caused a huge tsunami and sent poisonous gases into the air that killed the dinosaurs.

WHY DO OCEANS HAVE SALT WATER BUT RIVERS HAVE FRESH WATER?

The water in rivers comes from rain. Rainwater does not have any salt in it. The river picks up small amounts of salt from the ground as it travels downhill. This salt enters the ocean at the river mouth. The saltwater mixture becomes saltier as water evaporates.

ARE TIDAL WAVES AND TSUNAMIS THE SAME THING?

No, although many people confuse these two terms. The key is the word tidal. Tidal waves are just that—big waves that build up at high tide. A tsunami is a giant wave—or series of waves—caused by an underwater earthquake or volcanic eruption.

WHAT CAUSES OCEAN WAVES?

Wind passing over water creates waves. The water absorbs some of the wind's energy. However, the ocean's enormous water pressure pushes back up. These two opposite pushes create a wave movement that travels across the ocean.

ARE RAIN FORESTS ALWAYS IN HOT PLACES?

The most famous rain forests are in the hot tropical regions of South America, Africa, and Asia. But rain forests also develop in cooler parts of the world, as long as those places get enough rain. The Pacific coast of Canada has the largest temperate rain forest.

CAN A BUTTERFLY'S FLAPPING WING REALLY CAUSE A HURRICANE?

Maybe! The "butterfly effect" describes how a small change, such as the air movement caused by a butterfly's beating wings, can trigger much bigger changes. It works like a series of dominoes, where the first domino is tiny, and the last one is huge. This effect can make the weather very hard to predict.

WHERE ON EARTH IS THE EASIEST PLACE TO FORECAST THE WEATHER?

The British are always talking about the weather—because it's constantly changing. Other parts of the world, though, have much more constant climates. Probably the easiest place to forecast weather is the Atacama Desert in Chile, where no rain at all fell between 1571 and 1970.

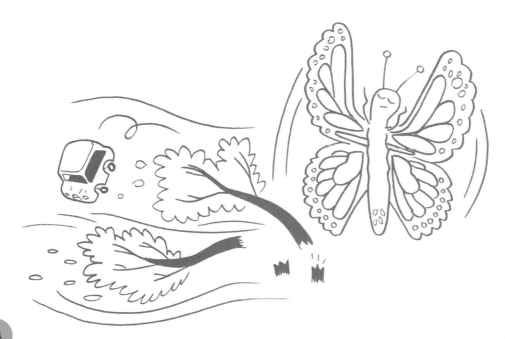

COULD A NUCLEAR EXPLOSION CHANGE THE EARTH'S ROTATION (SPINNING)?

Nuclear explosions release more energy than anything else that humans do. Luckily, the energy released by a nuclear explosion is only about one-trillionth of the energy of the Earth's spinning. Scientists compare it to trying to slow the speed of a truck by crashing it into a mosquito.

DO CORAL REEFS ONLY FORM IN TROPICAL WATERS?

Most coral reefs form in shallow tropical waters. However, scientists are now studying mysterious deep coral reefs, which can form in much colder waters. Coral reefs are under threat from pollution and fishing, so many people are working hard to protect them.

WHEN WILL WE RUN OUT OF OIL?

Nobody knows for sure. It is hard to say exactly how much oil is left or exactly how fast the world will use what it does find. Many experts believe that very little oil will be left after 2060. The world will need to find alternative sources of energy before then.

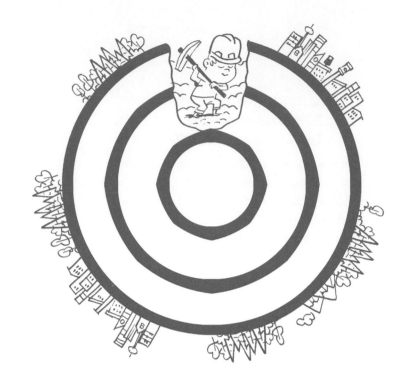

WHY DOESN'T THE HALF OF THE EARTH FACING AWAY FROM THE SUN FREEZE EVERY NIGHT?

We can thank our atmosphere for keeping us warm. The atmosphere stops most of the Sun's heat from radiating (escaping outward). It acts just like a snug blanket to keep us warm. The atmosphere also stops the Earth from getting too hot during the day.

WHAT'S IN THE MIDDLE OF THE EARTH?

The middle of the Earth is a ball of metal (nickel and iron). This is the inner core. It's the last layer that you would find if you peeled away the Earth's crust (the top layer), its mantle (sticky melted rock), and its outer core (liquid rock). The inner core is as hot as the Sun's surface—5,430°C (10,000°F).

HOW FAR FROM THE POLES CAN ICEBERGS GO BEFORE THEY MELT?

Most icebergs remain in the cold Arctic and Antarctic waters. But currents can take them into warmer areas. Icebergs are common off the Atlantic coast of Canada, and some Arctic icebergs drift as far south as Japan before melting.

WAS THE BIGGEST EXPLOSION IN EARTH'S HISTORY NATURAL OR MAN-MADE?

The largest man-made explosion was a Russian nuclear weapon exploded in 1961. However, the meteorite that crashed to Earth 65 million years ago and wiped out the dinosaurs made a bigger explosion. It was 1.7 million times more powerful than the Russian weapon.

WHY DO OUR EARS POP IN PLANES?

Inside our ears are tiny passages that are filled with air. Normally, this air has the same pressure (outward push) as the air all around us. As we go up in a plane, the air pressure around us gets weaker. But the air inside our ear passages is still the same. The ear has to let air out to change the pressure, and that's what makes our ears pop.

WHY DON'T CLOUDS FALL DOWN TO EARTH?

Clouds are made of millions of tiny drops of water and particles of ice. These are so small that they float in the air. Gravity can't pull them to the ground. But these small particles of ice and water can collide and form larger particles or drops. When they do, they fall to the ground as snow or rain.

HOW HIGH UP DOES THE ATMOSPHERE GO?

The atmosphere has five layers. The lowest layer, the troposphere, is where the weather changes. Above it is the stratosphere, where planes travel. Then there's the mesosphere—Earth's shield against meteors. The hot thermosphere is farther out and gives way to the thin exosphere. This layer finishes about 10,000 km (6,000 miles) above us.

WHAT MAKES THE WIND BLOW?

Some parts of the atmosphere are warmer than others. Cold air has a higher pressure than warm air (this means it pushes out harder). So cold air always tries to force its way into areas of warmer air. The wind we feel is air doing just that. If there's a big difference in air pressure, then the wind will be strong.

DO PLANES GET STRUCK BY LIGHTNING?

Passenger planes get hit by lightning about once a year. Luckily, the lightning usually has no bad effect on the plane or passengers. It just leaves a scorch mark where it first hits. The electrical charge travels along the outside of the plane. Most lightning strikes occur when planes are below 5 km (3 miles). Planes usually avoid trouble by flying higher than this.

WHY DO STALE COOKIES GET SOGGY BUT STALE BREAD GOES DRY?

Cookies start off dry and have less water than the air around them. Bread and cake have a little more water than the air around them. The water moves from where there's more to where there's less. That means it goes from the air into the cookies—making them soggy. And it goes from the bread into the air—making it drier.

WHY DOES POPCORN POP?

A popcorn kernel has an outer case with a starchy inside. There's usually a little water inside, too. When the kernel is heated enough, the water boils. The boiling water becomes a gas and suddenly expands. This "pops" the outer case and turns the kernel inside out. The yummy white fluffy parts are the starch.

HOW DOES YEAST MAKE BREAD RISE?

Yeast is a type of fungus that becomes active when it is warmed. Bakers mix it into bread dough. Then they leave it somewhere warm. The yeast begins to feed on the sugar in the dough. As it does, it gives off a gas that puffs up the dough and makes it rise.

WHY DO PLANTS GROW BETTER IN SOME SOILS THAN IN OTHERS?

Just like animals, plants need to take in food to grow and stay healthy. Minerals and other natural "plant foods" are called nutrients. Some soils have more nutrients than others, and some soils suit certain plants more than others.

HOW CAN YOU GET WORDS INTO CANDY?

British "rock" candy is made by boiling sugar until it looks like white modeling clay. As it cools, it is stretched into long strips. Some parts are dyed and pulled out into long string shapes. The clever part is arranging the dyed strings along the white strips to make words when the whole thing is rolled up. The thick roll is then stretched until it turns into a long piece of rock.

WHY IS THERE OFTEN A SPECIAL SMELL JUST BEFORE IT RAINS?

The smell is from a gas called ozone. High up in the atmosphere, a layer of ozone protects the Earth from harmful radiation. But the electricity in lightning can produce ozone nearer the ground. The ozone spreads out from rain clouds and often reaches you before the rain arrives.

WHAT HAPPENS WHEN PAPER IS RECYCLED?

Paper is made from wood pulp (wood that's mushed up). The first step of recycling is to add water to the old paper. That makes it easy to mush up and become pulp again. Then the pulp goes through a screen to get rid of ink, glue, and other fragments of material. It's then ready to become paper again.

COULD SOMEONE SQUEEZE A PIECE OF COAL AND TURN IT INTO DIAMOND, LIKE SUPERMAN?

Superman may have been able to do that trick, but it would never happen in nature. Both coal and diamond are made from a mineral called carbon. But they are very different. Coal started out as plants. Over millions of years, the dead plants were squished into coal. Diamonds formed even longer ago, at very high temperatures deep inside the Earth.

HOW DO SOLAR PANELS TURN SUNLIGHT INTO ELECTRICITY?

Both sunlight and electricity are made up of tiny objects called particles. The particles in sunlight are called photons. Electricity is a movement of particles called electrons. When photons of sunlight hit the silicon in a solar panel, they knock electrons off the silicon. Those electrons become an electric current.

CAN YOU REALLY HAMMER A NAIL WITH A BANANA?

Yes, if it's cold enough to be frozen solid. Scientists do this demonstration by dipping a banana into liquid nitrogen, which is extremely cold. Then they take the banana out and drive in a nail. You can even do this by leaving a banana outside overnight to get cold. Oh—the outside temperature needs to be −25°C (−13°F), though!

WHY DOES RUBBER STRETCH AND THEN POP BACK INTO SHAPE?

Rubber is made of long chains of molecules. These chains are held together in tight tangles, like a tangled string of Christmas lights. When you stretch the rubber, you straighten out those chains. But when you let go, they pop back to their original shape.

WHAT IS SMOKE?

Smoke is all the particles that aren't burned up in a fire. Only water and carbon dioxide are left behind when things are completely burned. But a fire can't burn everything if it doesn't have enough oxygen or if it hasn't become hot enough. So smoke is a mixture of tiny bits of solid, liquid, and gas that are all the leftovers, floating in the air.

HOW DO HUGE SHIPS FLOAT?

A huge object pushes away lots of water. If it's heavier than the water it pushes away, it will sink. If it's lighter than that water, it will float. A big ship is heavy, but not as heavy as that much water. It contains lots of empty spaces that are full of air.

WHY DON'T WE FEEL THE EARTH SPINNING?

The Earth rotates (spins) completely around once every 24 hours. That means that it's spinning at 1,670 km/h (1,070 mph). However, we don't feel that motion because we're also moving at the same speed. It's like flying in a plane—you don't feel like you're moving fast.

DOES ALL WOOD FLOAT?

Most wood floats because there's lots of air inside it between the wood cells. This makes wood weigh less than water—and float. Some types of wood, such as ebony, are very dense. That means their wood cells are packed so tightly there's not much room for air. These woods will sink in water.

HOW DO PARACHUTES WORK?

Skydivers are pulled toward Earth by gravity. But an upward force called air resistance pushes in the opposite direction. The large, flat shape of a parachute increases the amount of air resistance. The parachute is still pulled down by gravity, but because of the push of the air, it falls at a constant, slow speed.

COULD YOU SURVIVE IF YOU JUMPED UP JUST BEFORE A FALLING ELEVATOR HIT THE GROUND?

It wouldn't work, for two reasons. First, you'd never be able to jump up as fast as the elevator was falling down. Second, even if you could beat the speed of the fall, the elevator would still crash to the bottom. And that would mean the roof of the elevator would crush you as it passed.

CAN THE WIND REALLY DRIVE A STRAW THROUGH A TELEGRAPH POLE?

Yes, it can, if the wind is strong enough. Tornado winds blow at more than 500 km/h (300 mph), making harmless objects into deadly weapons. But isn't a straw too weak? Not if one end is blocked. Then the air rushes in and pushes out on the sides. The straw gets stronger, just like a pumped-up bike wheel.

HOW CAN SOME INSECTS WALK ACROSS WATER?

Water molecules are attracted to each other on all sides. But those on the surface have none above them. This makes them hold on to the ones beside them more strongly. And that hold creates a delicate film that can support light objects without breaking. Scientists call it surface tension.

IS THE SAYING "RED SKY AT NIGHT, SAILORS' DELIGHT" REALLY ACCURATE?

Yes, it often is. Rain clouds usually travel from west to east. They look red when the Sun is low. A "red sky at night" means that the Sun's rays are shining on clouds that have already passed to the east. This means that it is less likely to be stormy the next day.

WHY DO PEOPLE GET SEASICK?

Your brain receives signals from other parts of the body. They tell the brain whether you're moving or not. The signal for balance comes from inside your ear. On a rough sea, it tells your brain that you're going up and down. But your eyes see that the tables and walls on the ship aren't moving. Your brain gets confused, and the result is that awful feeling of seasickness.

WHY ARE SOAP BUBBLES ROUND?

Even if you blow a bubble through a square wand, the bubble is still round. Weird, huh? It happens like this. When you blow through the wand, the bubble forms with air inside. The shape that uses the least energy to form is a sphere (a round shape). So even if it starts off as a long sausage shape while you blow, your bubble will always end up round.

WHY DO CLOTHES DRY ON A CLOTHESLINE EVEN WHEN THE SUN ISN'T OUT?

Because the water in the wet clothes evaporates. The molecules in a liquid are constantly crashing into each other. They pass energy along with each crash. Some molecules wind up with enough energy to break free of the liquid and become a gas. This is evaporation—and it's how your clothes get dry.

HOW DO NONSTICK PANS WORK?

Here's an example of chemistry helping you out in everyday life. The inside of the pan is covered in a layer of Teflon. That brand name is easier to say than the official chemical name of this substance—polytetrafluoroethylene. Teflon does not react with other substances, which means that things don't stick to it.

HOW DOES VELCRO WORK?

Velcro is simple. It has two pieces. One has lots and lots of small plastic hooks. The other piece has loads of tiny loops made of string. The hooks fit into the loops when the pieces go together. Velcro is strong because there are so many locking hooks and loops.

WHY DO MAGNETS PICK UP SOME THINGS AND NOT OTHERS?

Magnets can only affect other magnets. What makes something magnetic? Inside any substance, you will find tiny specks of matter called electrons. In a magnetic substance, such as iron, some of those electrons aren't linked to any other electrons, and they can line up to form loads of "mini magnets." But in substances that aren't magnetic, all the electrons are linked to each other. They cancel out each other's possible magnetic force.

HOW DOES GLUE MAKE THINGS STICK TOGETHER?

Scientists can't agree on the whole explanation! They know that most glues start off as liquids and finish as solids. To work well, they need to seep into dips and ridges on the things they're attaching. Once they've become solids, the two things are held together. But scientists will have to look more and more closely—down to the tiny level of atoms and beyond—to figure out why the glue really sticks.

CAN STAINLESS STEEL RUST?

Steel is a mixture of iron and carbon. It is strong, but it rusts in much the same way as iron itself. If you add chromium, you produce stainless steel. Chromium gives stainless steel its shine. It also provides a barrier to stop oxygen from getting at the steel. Without oxygen, the chemical reaction that produces rust cannot take place.

WHY DOES OIL MAKE TOOLS LAST LONGER?

The metal parts of tools look smooth, but their edges are uneven. When they move against each other, these uneven parts catch. The tool doesn't work so well, and the moving parts wear down. Oil keeps those parts from touching each other. They can still move back and forth, but they don't catch anymore.

HOW FAST DOES A GLACIER MOVE?

Scientists often describe glaciers as being "rivers of ice." Like normal rivers, glaciers flow at different speeds. It depends on the slope of the land, the air temperature, the soil beneath, and many other factors. The fastest, Greenland's Quarayaq glacier, travels up to 24 m (80 feet) a day.

WHY DOES A RAZOR BLADE GET BLUNT IF IT ONLY HAS TO CUT HAIR?

You'd have to look closely—really closely—at the blade to find out. A human hair is harder to cut than copper wire of the same size. It knocks atoms off the edge of the blade when the razor hits it. Lots of hairs knock lots of atoms off. And without the straight line of atoms forming an edge, the blade gets dull and blunt.

WHY DOES OLD PAPER TURN YELLOW?

Paper is made of wood. The part of wood called cellulose makes paper white. But wood also contains a dark substance called lignin. This adds strength to wood. In time, the lignin in paper breaks down and forms yellow acids. And it's these that turn the paper yellow.

CAN YOU STICK TWO BOOKS TOGETHER WITHOUT USING GLUE?

Yes, and the secret comes from the force of friction. Face the open pages of two paperback books toward each other. Slowly fan the pages, so that the pages of each book extend about 5 cm (2 in) into the other. Now try to pull them apart. It's hard because the force of friction builds up with each overlap.

WHY DOES A COAT HANGER BREAK IF YOU BEND IT BACK AND FORTH?

It's all because of something called metal fatigue. Fatigue means "tiredness," and that's a good description of what happens. Bending the metal back and forth opens up tiny cracks in the surface of the metal. The cracks get wider and wider until ... the hanger breaks.

WHY IS GRASS GREEN NOT BLUE?

Grass uses light from the Sun to create the energy it needs to survive and grow. This energy-producing process is called photosynthesis. It relies on a chemical found in plants called chlorophyll, which is green!

ARE TOMATOES FRUITS OR VEGETABLES?

Even some scientists disagree about this. The simple answer is that tomatoes are fruits. Why? Because scientists define a fruit as the mature ovary of a plant that contains seeds. All the other parts of a plant—such as leaves (e.g. lettuce), stems (e.g. celery), and roots (e.g. carrots), are called vegetables.

CAN YOU EAT FLOWERS?

You certainly can! In fact, you may have eaten some this week if you've had broccoli or cauliflower. These are the flowering parts of plants. Many attractive flowers, such as violets and roses, can also be eaten or used to make teas. But it's important to remember that some flowers are poisonous, and we should never simply assume that a flower is edible.

WHAT IS THE LARGEST FRUIT IN THE WORLD?

The jackfruit tree produces a fruit that weighs more than a ten-year-old child. It grows in the rain forests of India and Southeast Asia. The fruits can be 90 cm (36 in) long, 47 cm (19 in) wide, and can weigh 36 kg (80 lb). They taste like a banana, but are more sour.

ARE PEANUTS REALLY NUTS?

No. Peanuts are the seeds of legumes—members of a plant family that includes beans. Legume fruits form hard shells known as pods, which contain two or more seeds. Peas—which everyone knows grow in pods—are also legumes. Almonds and walnuts are true nuts. They are the one-seeded fruit of full-sized trees and grow inside a hard shell.

IS IT REALLY POSSIBLE TO DRIVE A CAR THROUGH A TREE?

Yes. In the giant redwood and sequoia forests of northern California, there are several trees that have been hollowed out so that cars can drive through them. One of the most famous is 96 m (315 ft) tall. A road passes through a hole in the trunk that is 1.83 m (6 ft) wide and 2.06 m (6 ft 9 in) high.

WHAT'S THE "POINT" OF THORNS?

Plants have no way of escaping from hungry animals looking for tasty leaves or blossoms for their next meal. That's why some plants, such as roses and cacti, grow thorns to protect themselves. A deer might think twice about sticking its delicate nose through a bunch of thorns just to reach a tasty rosebud.

WHICH PLANT HAS THE LARGEST SEEDS?

The world's largest seed comes from the Coco de Mer. This is a type of palm tree that is native to islands in the Indian Ocean. Its seeds form inside giant egg-shaped fruit. These can weigh more than 17 kg (37 lb).

CAN CORN REALLY GROW "AS HIGH AS AN ELEPHANT'S EYE"?

This is a line from a famous American song—but is it just a tall tale? Most elephants' eyes are about 3 m (10 ft) off the ground, and most corn is harvested when it is about 2.5 m (8 ft) tall. But with enough rain, sunshine, and fertilizer, corn can grow up to 4 m (13 ft) or even higher. So in fact, corn can grow even taller than an elephant's eye!

WHY DO NETTLES STING?

Nettles sting for the same reason that some plants have thorns: To protect themselves. Nettle flowers are protected from plant-eating mammals by the stinging leaves all around them. However, insects are still able to land on the flowers and carry away their pollen, so that the nettles can reproduce.

DO A TREE'S ROOTS GROW AS DEEP DOWNWARD AS THE TREE GROWS UPWARD?

Most tree roots are surprisingly shallow. Even some of the tallest trees have roots that go down less than 45 cm (18 in). Trees can be blown over in strong winds because they don't have deep roots to anchor them. Although the roots are shallow, they can be wide. Some root networks are three times as wide as the branches above.

WHY DO TREES HAVE BARK?

Trees and shrubs actually have two layers of bark. The inner layer is made up of long, tubelike cells called xylem. They transport water and minerals up from the roots. The outer layer is made up of dead cells. These cells have hardened to form a protective barrier against insects. They also keep water from evaporating from the inner bark.

DO MEXICAN JUMPING BEANS REALLY JUMP?

Yes, they really do bounce, but they're not really beans, and it's not the plant that's doing the jumping. The larva of a small moth eats into the seed casing of a Mexican shrub. Protected from the desert sun, it grows into an adult moth. But if it feels too warm inside, it swings to try and move into the shade. And that makes the "bean" seem to jump.

WHAT IS THE SMELLIEST FRUIT?

The durian grows in Southeast Asia and looks a little bit like a large, thorny pineapple. But its smell is what makes the durian famous. It's been described as a cross between rotten onions and dirty gym socks! Some people actually like the smell and describe the durian as the "king of fruits."

WHY DO SOME CACTI ONLY BLOOM FOR ONE DAY A YEAR?

The purple ball cactus needs to attract insects to its flowers in order to reproduce. However, a delicate bloom like a rose or tulip would shrivel in the desert heat. The cactus solves this problem by making a flower with a protective waxy covering. However, it takes a lot of effort to make this flower ... so much so that it only blooms for one day a year!

WHY ARE CARROTS ORANGE?

Until the late 1600s, carrots could be purple, white, red, or yellow. According to one theory, today's orange carrots are descendants of the "Long Orange Dutch Carrot," which was first described in 1721. This was created by Dutch farmers who were looking for a way to commemorate their leader, William of Orange. They crossbred different carrot varieties until they found a hardy orange variety.

WHICH PLANTS DID THE FIRST HUMAN FARMERS GROW?

Scientists are looking for evidence of when humans first began farming. In 2006, scientists uncovered a collection of figs and human remains in Israel that was 11,300 years old. The figs were a type that needed to be planted—not just picked. Another recent find, in Korea, suggests that farmers might have been growing rice 15,000 years ago.

WHY ARE BONSAI TREES SO SMALL?

Bonsai is the Japanese art of producing small trees and shrubs to look like fully grown trees. Their owners trim and prune small branches to make them grow in this unusual way. Most bonsai (meaning "tray-planted") trees are only about 50 cm (20 in) tall.

CAN PLANTS GROW AT THE NORTH OR SOUTH POLES?

No plants can grow at the North or South Poles because the temperatures are so cold all year. A few plants manage to survive in the Arctic region near the North Pole and the Antarctic region near the South Pole. These tend to be simple plants such as moss or tough grasses.

WHAT ARE GM CROPS?

Some scientists are working to alter the genes in plants to make them more productive or better able to resist pests. Plants that have been modified (changed) like this are called genetically modified (GM) crops. But there's a big debate about the effects of GM crops on the environment.

DOES A CACTUS HAVE ANY LEAVES?

Its leaves, called spines, look like sharp needles. A leaf shaped like an oak or beech leaf would shrivel up in the hot desert sun. The spines protect the cactus against plant-eating animals.

ARE GREEN POTATOES REALLY POISONOUS?

Green potatoes contain a poison called solanine, which makes you feel sick and gives you bad headaches. Potatoes make solanine when they are exposed to warmth and light. Warmth and light also lead the potato to produce chlorophyll. So it's the green chlorophyll that's the clue that there is poison in the potato.

WHY ARE THERE NO TREES ON MOUNT EVEREST AND OTHER HIGH MOUNTAINS?

The air temperature goes down the higher up you climb. The temperature on the highest mountains is around -40° C (-40° F) . High winds, even on lower mountains, blow soil away, so that only rock remains. These conditions are no good for plants.

DO PLANTS GROW ON ANY OTHER PLANETS?

So far, scientists have found no evidence of any type of life on other planets. Most are either too hot or too cold. NASA scientists have sent a robot vehicle called Curiosity to study Mars. It might find evidence that plants did grow there long ago, when the planet's atmosphere was more like ours.

COULD A PLANT GROW IN YOUR STOMACH IF YOU SWALLOWED A SEED?

Luckily, this is not a problem. Think about what plants need to survive—water, carbon dioxide, light, and nutrients from soil. Of these, only water could be available in your stomach, and even then, it would be mixed with strong acid. So the conditions just aren't right for growing plants in your stomach.

WHERE DOES CHOCOLATE COME FROM?

Chocolate comes from the beans (or "seeds") of the cacao tree. These beans are left in pots to ferment and become less bitter. Then they are roasted and their outer shells are removed. What's left, the "nibs," are crushed into a paste. Chocolate makers then mix in sugar, vanilla, and often milk. The paste is mashed for days and then heated several times. The result is delicious chocolate.

DOES SPINACH REALLY MAKE YOU STRONG?

For years, people believed that spinach made you strong because it contains a lot of iron (which strengthens muscles). In reality, spinach has no more iron than most other green vegetables. It is still good for you, though. The vitamins it contains protect the heart, bones, and eyes.

CAN YOU REALLY SIT ON A LILY PAD?

You can't sit on just any water lily, but some tropical species are large enough to hold a young child. The giant water lily of the Amazon region produces more than 40 leaves, which rest on the calm water surface. The leaves grow up to 2.5 m (8 ft) across and can support up to 45 kg (100 lb) without sinking.

IS SEAWEED A PLANT?

The answer is "almost." Seaweed is a type of algae. Like plants, it can create its own food using photosynthesis. Unlike plants, seaweed has no roots or tubes running through it to deliver food and water. That's because every part of it is touching water and able to make food, so there's no need for a system of "pipes,"

WHY DO FARMERS FLOOD RICE FIELDS?

Water is an important part of rice-growing. Filling a field with a shallow layer of water for a few days, and then draining it, kills off weeds and other pests. Luckily, the rice can survive this three-day bath, so it continues to grow.

WHY DOES A PLANT DIE IF YOU OVERWATER IT?

All plants need some water to survive and grow, but they will die if they have too much. This is because plant roots need to be able to absorb gases from the air. They do not work properly if they are underwater because they can't send water and nutrients to the rest of the plant. More houseplants die from overwatering than from lack of water.

DOES POISON ALWAYS TASTE BAD?

No. Sometimes poisonous things can taste good. People sometimes eat mushrooms and then find out that they're poisonous. And some things that smell or taste bad are really good for you. You should always be sure of what you eat.

ARE MUSHROOMS PLANTS?

They grow on the ground. People eat them. Mushrooms must be plants, right? The answer is no! Mushrooms lack one of the most important features of plants—the ability to make their own food. Instead, mushrooms feed on dead and decaying plants, which is why we see them on old tree stumps.

WHY ARE MOTHS ATTRACTED TO LIGHT?

Moths use the Moon to help guide them at night. Bright lights—such as electric lights or candles—look a lot like the Moon, and this confuses them. As they fly along, they seem to be moving past the Moon, which shouldn't be possible! They keep changing direction to try to fly straight. But instead, they fly closer and closer to the light.

HOW CAN BIRDS SIT ON POWER LINES WITHOUT BEING KILLED?

The birds survive because the electricity in the power lines has no reason to pass through them. A copper wire is easier to pass through than a bird, so the electricity stays in the wire. However, the birds could die if they were touching the wire at the same time as touching something else.

HOW DOES GPS WORK?

GPS stands for "Global Positioning System." At least 24 satellites are orbiting Earth and sending down information. A car's GPS system constantly receives information from several satellites. Its computer uses that information to figure out exactly where you are—your "global position." It then compares it with where you want to be. Then it tells you how to reach your destination.

WHY IS IT HARD TO WALK UPHILL?

Simple, really—it's all because of gravity. That's the force that draws everything toward the core of the Earth. Gravity helps if you're walking or riding your bike downhill because it's pulling in the right direction. Going uphill, though, means working against the same force.

WHY DO PEOPLE LIVE LONGER THAN THEY DID IN THE PAST?

People in Ancient Rome had an average life span of just 28 years. These days, the average world life expectancy has risen to 71 years, and in the United States, most people can expect to live to about 78. This is because we now have better food and medicine to fight disease. Also, people know how important it is to stay clean in order to stop the spread of germs.

IS THERE A LIMIT TO HOW FAST ATHLETES CAN RUN?

Top athletes today are much faster than runners of 100 or even 30 years ago. That's largely because of better food and improved training. There's probably a limit to how fast even the best athlete can go—but we still have many things to find out about what happens in the legs and feet when an athlete runs.

WHY ARE SOME PEOPLE LEFT-HANDED?

Whether you are left- or right-handed is partly controlled by your genes. It's also linked to human development over thousands of years. Scientists believe that being right-handed helped early humans build many skills, such as writing. But left-handed people still had some advantages in fighting and hunting.

DOES YOUR WEIGHT VARY DURING THE DAY?

Most people weigh less first thing in the morning than at other times of day. It's mainly because of water. At night, you lose a lot of water as you breathe out and sweat. Then you go to the bathroom when you wake up. Getting rid of all of this water means you lose a bit of weight. During the day, you drink and your weight goes back up again.

WHICH PART OF THE WORLD HAS THE TALLEST PEOPLE?

The tallest humans are among the groups of people living by the River Nile in East Africa. It is common to see men almost 2 m (6 foot 8 inches) tall. If you have tall parents, you are likely to be tall, too—although what you eat and your lifestyle are also important.

DOES EATING FISH MAKE YOU CLEVER?

This advice seemed like a fairy tale for many years. Now scientists believe it is true. People who eat some types of fish (such as tuna and mackerel) do score better on tests. These fish contain a fatty acid called omega-3, which helps more blood flow to your brain.

WHAT IS A TEST-TUBE BABY?

Babies develop after a father's sperm cell joins with a mother's egg cell. Normally, that happens in a tube inside the mother's body. Sometimes the tube is damaged and the sperm can't reach the egg. So scientists remove sperm cells and eggs to join them together in a test tube. The new unborn baby (the embryo) is put back inside the mother's womb to develop normally.

CAN WE INHERIT THE ABILITY TO SPEAK FRENCH OR DO DIFFICULT CALCULATIONS?

No one is born with the ability to speak a foreign language or to figure out difficult equations. But people can inherit talents that make it easier for them to learn those skills. It's the same with sports. No one is born a football player or tennis star. But some people find it easier to become good at these sports.

WHY DO WE DREAM?

We all dream, even if we can't remember our dreams in the morning. But doctors can't agree why we dream. Some say that dreams have no real purpose. Others believe that they are a way of dealing with problems that trouble us when we're awake.

WHY DO CHILDREN HAVE TO GO TO BED BEFORE GROWN-UPS?

Children need to go to bed earlier and get more sleep than adults for two reasons. One is to help the body build up its energy. Growing uses up lots of energy. The other is that sleep itself helps the brain. Scientists believe that a child's brain needs sleep to develop.

WHAT CAUSES SLEEPWALKING?

We all pass through different stages of sleep each night. Sometimes we are disturbed slightly in a "deep sleep" stage. We seem to wake up and begin to mumble or even walk. But we're still asleep. Sleepwalking is most common in children, and most outgrow it by the time they are teenagers.

AMAZING ANIMALS

HOW STRONG ARE RATS?
Rats are so tough that they can fall from the fifth floor of a building and walk away unharmed.

HOW LONG DO A RAT'S TEETH GROW?
A rat's tooth grow continuously during its life. If it didn't keep chewing, its lower teeth would eventually grow through its top jaw and through the roof of its mouth.

DO RAT TAILS GET TANGLED?
Rats that hibernate together sometimes get their tails tied up in a big knot. If the rats urinate over themselves in the winter, they can freeze together in a block!

HOW MANY BUGS DO BATS EAT?

Just a single bat can eat between 3,000 and 7,000 mosquitoes in a night. A colony of 500 of the flying fiends can munch their way through a quarter of a million bugs in an hour.

WHAT USE IS BAT POOP?

Bracken Cave in Texas, USA, is home to 20 million bats. The floor is caked in a thick layer of bat feces that the locals collect to use as fertilizer.

DID YOU KNOW?

Vampire bats are surprisingly thoughtful. If a bat is too ill to go out and feed, another bat will suck blood all night, come home, and vomit it over the sick bat so that it doesn't miss out on a meal. How kind!

WHY DOES A SKINK LOSE ITS TAIL?

The Polynesian skink (a small lizard) has a bright blue tail which it can shed if it is attacked. The tail continues wriggling after the lizard has gone, keeping the predator distracted.

HOW DO CHAMELEONS CATCH BUGS?

Some chameleons have long tongues with a sticky, goo-covered lump on the end that they shoot out to snatch insects.

HOW DO CROCODILES EAT?

Crocodiles can't chew their food. Instead, they hold their prey and then twist their bodies and teeth around it to tear off chunks of flesh.

HOW CAREFUL IS AN ELEPHANT'S TRUNK?

As well as uprooting trees, an elephant's trunk can perform delicate operations such as plucking a single blade of grass from the ground.

HOW MANY TEETH DOES AN ELEPHANT HAVE?

An elephant has four functional teeth, each one being 30 cm (12 in) long. They are replaced six times in a lifetime, but after the last replacement the elephant can no longer eat properly.

IS AN ELEPHANT A NOISY EATER?

An elephant's tummy makes so much noise when it's digesting food that if there's any danger of a predator hearing it, it can immediately stop digesting. Ingenious! Try it yourself!

IS THERE A FROG THAT'S SMALLER THAN ITS TADPOLE?

When it is a tadpole, the paradoxical frog of South America can grow to 25 cm (10 in), but then it shrinks to only 6 cm (2.4 in) when it becomes a fully grown frog!

HOW HARD IS A HEAD BUTT FROM A MOUNTAIN GOAT?

During mating competitions, Montana mountain goats can butt heads so hard that the shock can cause their hooves to fall off.

WHAT IS THE ODDEST SOUND MADE BY A FROG?

In winter, the croak of a golden tree frog sounds like a mallet chipping away at a rock, but in summer, it sounds like a tinkling bell!

HOW DO POLAR BEARS FIND FOOD?

Polar bears use their sense of smell to track down prey up to 30 km (18 miles) away. Even thick ice doesn't stop them from tracking their prey.

HOW BIG IS A POLAR BEAR'S BELLY?

The polar bear has the largest stomach capacity (in relation to its size) of any animal. It can kill and eat a large walrus or even a beluga whale.

IS A POLAR BEAR WHITE UNDER ITS FUR?

The skin under a polar bear's white fur is actually black!

HOW DO POLAR BEARS STOP THEIR FEET FROM GETTING COLD?

Polar bears are the only mammals with hair on the soles of their feet.

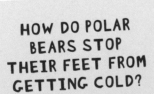

WHAT IS THE WORLD'S FASTEST REPTILE?

The fastest reptile on the planet is the spiny-tailed iguana from Costa Rica, clocking in at a foot-burning 35 km/h (22 mph).

HOW STRONG IS A GILA MONSTER BITE?

The bite of a Gila monster (a large venomous lizard) is so strong that the only way to detach one, once it has bitten, is to drown it.

HOW DOES A POSSUM PLAY DEAD?

A possum "plays dead" if it feels threatened. It lies completely still, hangs its tongue out, leaks dung, and oozes green slime that smells like rotten flesh.

WHICH SNAKE IS THE DEADLIEST?

Carpet vipers kill more people than any other type of snake; their bite leads to uncontrollable bleeding.

HOW DANGEROUS IS A KING COBRA'S VENOM?

The venom of the king cobra is so deadly that 1 g (0.04 oz) of it can kill 150 people. Just handling the substance with bare skin can put a person in a coma.

DID YOU KNOW?

A rattlesnake's venom remains poisonous up to 25 years after it has died.

HOW OFTEN DOES A PYTHON NEED TO EAT?

A python can live for around six months without eating anything.

WHAT'S THE SCARIEST-LOOKING ANIMAL?

The aye-aye (a nocturnal mammal from Madagascar) has one very long, bony finger on one hand. It looks so scary that people used to believe they would die if they came into contact with one.

HOW MUCH DOES A BLACK RHINO POOP?

The African black rhinoceros excretes its own weight in dung every 48 hours. That's 682 kg (1,500 lb) a day.

IS A DUCKBILLED PLATYPUS A REAL ANIMAL?

Yes, but when staff at London's British Museum first saw one, they thought it was a fake animal and tried to pull off its bill!

HOW LONG DOES IT TAKE A SLOTH TO EAT ITS DINNER?

The contents of a sloth's stomach can take up to a month to be digested completely. That's a lot of rotten twigs and berries!

WHY DOESN'T MY CAT ROAR?

Members of the cat family can either roar or purr—they can't do both. The ones that can roar are lions, jaguars, tigers, and leopards.

HOW LOUD IS A LION'S ROAR?

An adult lion's roar is so loud that it can be heard up to 8 km (5 miles) away.

DO ANY ANIMALS HAVE THREE EYES?

The tuatara lizard of New Zealand has two normal eyes and a third placed neatly on the top of its head!

HOW LONG WOULD IT TAKE TO FILL A SWIMMING POOL WITH MILK?

That depends on how many cows you have! It would take a year of milking 330 cows to gather the 2,575 metric tons (660,253 gallons) of the white stuff you would need to fill an Olympic-sized swimming pool.

DO SQUIRRELS REMEMBER WHERE THEY BURY ALL THEIR NUTS?

Even though they spend most of the year hiding them for winter, most squirrels can't remember where they hide half of their nuts.

WHICH ANIMAL IS THE BRAINIEST?

In relation to body size, tree shrews have the largest brain of any animal.

WHAT DO YOU CALL A GROUP OF RHINOS?

The collective name for a group of rhinoceros is a "crash." Very appropriate!

HOW LOUD IS A HOWLER MONKEY?

The call of the male howler monkey can be heard up to 16 km (10 miles) away. That's twice as far as a lion's roar!

WHO HAS THE BEST MEMORY, A CAT OR DOG?

Cats have better memories than dogs. Tests have concluded that a dog's short-term memory lasts no more than five minutes; a cat's can last as long as 16 hours.

HOW MANY DIFFERENT SOUNDS CAN CATS AND DOGS MAKE?

Cats can make over 100 vocal sounds, while dogs can make only ten.

105-3120A
Assault and Cattery

HAVE CATS EVER BEEN ARRESTED?

In 2006, Lewis the cat was put under house arrest by police in Connecticut, USA, because of his unprovoked attacks on local people. He was even placed in a line-up and picked out as the guilty party by a number of his victims.

HOW DO HAMSTERS REMEMBER THEIR ROUTE HOME?

When in unfamiliar territory, a hamster will rub its scent glands (found along its sides) against various objects. This leaves a scent trail the hamster can follow to go the other way!

WHAT DO HAMSTERS EAT IN THE WILD?

In the wild, a hamster's winter food store can be huge. Some contain over 1.5 million seeds!

HOW FAR DOES A HAMSTER RUN ON A WHEEL?

On average, a hamster will run up to 9.6 km (6 miles) a night on an exercise wheel.

WHICH BIRDS FLY THE FARTHEST?

The Arctic tern flies a round trip of 35,000 km (21,750 miles) a year, breeding in the Arctic in the northern summer and feeding in the Antarctic during the southern summer. The bar-tailed godwit migrates farther in a single trip than any other bird. Each year it travels non-stop from Alaska to New Zealand in just nine days and loses over half of its body weight on the trip.

DO BIRDS WEAR SUNGLASSES?

Some sea birds, such as gulls and terns, have red oil in their eyes. This acts like a pair of sunglasses that protect their eyes from the glare of bright sunlight.

WHICH BIRD HAS THE BIGGEST VOCABULARY?

A budgerigar by the name of Puck has the largest animal vocabulary, entering the Guinness Book of World Records in 1995 with a hefty 1,728 words.

HOW SENSITIVE ARE A CAT'S WHISKERS?

Cats' whiskers can detect movements 2,000 times smaller than the width of a human hair.

CAN YOU TRAIN CATS TO DO JOBS?

Thirty-seven cats were employed to carry bundles of letters to villages in Liège, Belgium, in 1879. The cats proved pretty undisciplined and the service didn't last long. Yet the creators seemed surprised at the failure!

WHY IS CAT FOOD NOT MADE OF MICE?

Pet food manufacturers once developed a mousey cat food, but cats just didn't like the taste.

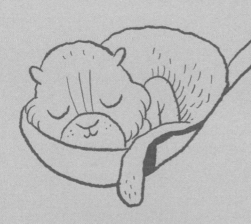

WHICH AMAZON FISH IS SCARIER THAN A PIRANHA?

The candiru (an eel-like fish) lives in the Amazon River and is more feared than the piranha. The transparent fish can smell pee in the water and heads straight for the source. It enters the body of its victim and burrows toward a major blood vessel to feed.

HOW BIG IS A BABY FERRET?

A newborn ferret is so small that it can fit on a teaspoon.

IS THERE A CURE FOR DOG POOP?

To solve the problem of dog poop left on city streets, Dutch scientists developed a dog food that is almost entirely absorbed by dogs, leaving only 10 percent waste. Dogs eating the new food produce only a small, dry pellet of poop.

HOW MANY BABIES DO RABBITS HAVE?

The largest rabbit litter on record contained 24 babies. The average number of rabbits in a litter is about six!

WHAT IS THE SMALLEST BREED OF CAT?

Weighing only 1.8 kg (4 lb), the Singapura is the smallest breed of domestic cat. That's the same weight as a medium-sized pineapple.

WHAT IS THE HEAVIEST-EVER DOG?

The heaviest dog on record is an old English mastiff named Zorba, who weighed 155 kg (343 lb). That's the same as two adult male humans.

WHERE DOES THE SAYING "RAINING CATS AND DOGS" COME FROM?

During heavy downpours in seventeenth-century England, many stray cats and dogs would float down the narrow streets.

HAS A DOG EVEN BEEN INTO SPACE?

Laika the dog was the world's first astronaut. She was sent into space by the Russian government aboard a satellite in 1957.

DID LAIKA SURVIVE?

Laika was also the world's first space casualty after dying from stress and overheating a few hours after take-off.

CAN DOGS FLY?

A dog named Brutus became the world's highest-skydiving dog in 1997 after making a jump of 1,393 m (4,572 ft).

HOW LONG DO GOLDFISH LIVE FOR?

A goldfish can live for over 40 years.

DO PEOPLE PREFER THEIR PETS OVER HUMANS?

In a pet-insurance survey, more than 50 percent of pet owners said they would rather be stranded on a desert island with their pet than with another person.

ARE CATS LAZY?

Cats are among the laziest animals, sleeping up to 18 hours a day. Cats fall asleep quickly but wake up frequently to check that their environment is safe from predators. That's where the term "cat nap" comes from, meaning a short snooze.

HOW WELL DO RABBITS TASTE?

A rabbit's tongue contains 17,000 taste buds. That's over 7,000 more than an average human!

WHAT DO BABY BUNNIES SMELL LIKE?

Baby bunnies have no smell at all, which helps protect them from predators.

DO PEOPLE EAT GUINEA PIGS?

Guinea pig meat is always on the menu in Peru and Bolivia where the animals are bred as food.

ARE THERE ANY DOG MILLIONAIRES?

The USA is home to some very pampered pooches, with an estimated 1 million dogs having been named as the main beneficiary in their owners' wills! When Ella Wendel from New York died in 1931 she left a fortune of US$30 million/£22,464,000 to her beloved dog Toby— her pet poodle!

HOW WELL DO DOGS SMELL?

A dog's sense of smell is one of the most advanced in the world. If a stew was cooking, a human would smell the overall aroma, whereas a dog would smell all of the ingredients individually. A dog has up to 150 sq cm (23 sq in) of olfactory membrane—the area in the brain used to detect smells. A human has just 4 sq cm (0.62 sq in).

HOW MANY MICE CAN A CAT CATCH?

The largest number of mice caught by a single cat is 28,899 over a 24-year period. That's about four mice a day, every day!

IS EATING MICE GOOD FOR CATS?

A cat would have to eat five mice to gain the same nutritional value as the average canned or dry cat food.

CAN DOGS ANSWER THE PHONE?

No, but around 30 percent of US pet owners admit to talking to their dogs or leaving messages on their answering machines for their dogs while they are away.

HOW MUCH DOES IT COST TO LOOK AFTER A DOG?

Based on an average life span of 11 years, the cost of owning a dog is US$13,350 or £9,991.

WHAT JOB WERE POODLES BRED TO DO?

Poodles were originally used in Europe as hunting dogs. Imagine!

HOW MUCH DO COWS DROOL?

Cows produce 200 times more saliva than humans. Never ask a cow to blow out the candles on your birthday cake!

WHAT IS THE HEAVIEST-EVER CAT?

The heaviest cat on record was Himmy, an Australian cat, who weighed 21.3 kg (46.8 lb). No other cat has weighed so much since!

ARE SOME PEOPLE AFRAID OF CATS?

Ailurophobia is a fear of cats. Julius Caesar, Henry II, Charles XI, and Napoleon were all sufferers and would nearly faint in the presence of a cat.

DID YOU KNOW?

Customs officials at Melbourne Airport, Australia, were suspicious when they heard splashing sounds coming from a woman's skirt. It turned out she was smuggling 51 live tropical fish in a water-filled apron!

HOW DO YOU HYPNOTIZE A CHICKEN?

You can hypnotize a chicken by repeatedly drawing a line on the ground in front of it . The chicken will stay in the same spot as long as you keep drawing the line!

IS A BALD EAGLE REALLY BALD?

Not really. It actually has white feathers on its head, neck, and tail. The "bald" part comes from the Old English word balde, meaning "white."

HOW STRONG ARE BALD EAGLES?

Bald eagles can fly carrying 2–3 kg (4–7 lb) of food in their talons. Try carrying four bags of sugar to see how heavy it is!

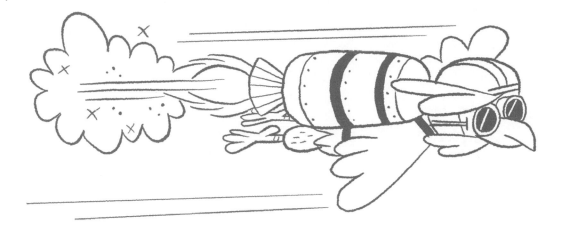

CAN CHICKENS FLY?

Yes, but not very far! The longest recorded flight for a chicken is 13 seconds.

CAN BIRDS GET TOO FULL TO FLY?

Vultures sometimes eat so much that they become too heavy to fly. They have to vomit to bring their weight down.

WHY DON'T DUCKS GET FROZEN FEET IN WINTER?

Ducks' feet contain no nerves or blood vessels. This means they never feel the cold when they swim in icy water.

DO BIRDS PLAY FOOTBALL?

Turkeys and chickens like to play with objects and toss them around. No word on the first chicken football team yet, though!

HOW DO VULTURES HELP HUMANS?

American turkey vultures help humans detect broken underground fuel pipes. The leaking fuel smells like carrion (the dead animals they eat). The clusters of birds standing around leaks show the engineers where repairs are needed.

HOW DOES A TURKEY VULTURE KEEP COOL?

The turkey vulture covers its legs in poop to keep cool when it is hot.

DO ALL PENGUINS LIVE AT THE SOUTH POLE?

Not all penguins live in cold climates—the Galápagos penguin lives near the Equator in temperatures of up to 29°C/84°F.

CAN BIRDS SLEEP IN THE AIR?

The sooty tern only lands to breed and rear its young. It eats, sleeps, and drinks while flying and can stay airborne for ten years! An albatross also sleeps while it flies! It can doze while cruising at 40 km/h (25 mph).

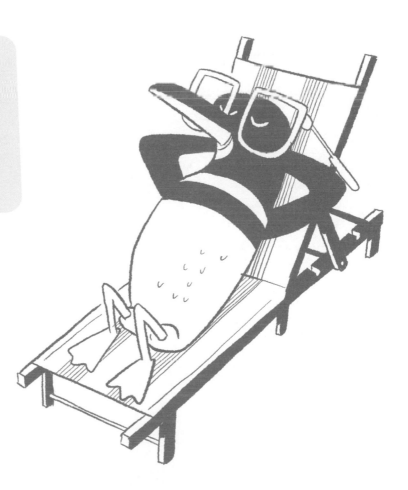

CAN PENGUINS FLY?

Penguins can jump nearly 3 m (10 ft) into the air ... but they can't fly!

75

HOW MANY WORMS DOES A CHICK EAT?

If you laid end to end all the earthworms eaten by a baby robin in one day, they would stretch to 4 m (13 ft).

CAN BABY BIRDS CLIMB TREES?

Hoatzin chicks from South America can. They use special claws to move around until their wings are strong enough for them to fly.

WHAT IS AN OWL PELLET?

Owls swallow their prey (mostly mice and voles) whole. The parts they cannot digest, like fur and bones, are formed into small pellets that the owl vomits up.

HOW MANY INSECTS ARE THERE ON EARTH?

There are around 1.4 billion insects for every one human on Earth.

IS A TARANTULA HAWK A SPIDER OR A BIRD?

Neither! The tarantula hawk is actually a wasp. The female wasp attacks and paralyzes a tarantula spider before laying an egg in its body. The hatched wasp then eats the tarantula alive as its first meal.

HOW DO YOU TURN A COCKROACH INTO A ZOMBIE?

The female jewel wasp can turn a cockroach into a "zombie" by stinging it in the head. The cockroach lies paralyzed while the wasp lays its eggs in its body, dying only when the hatched wasp larva chews its way out of the cockroach's stomach.

HOW DO SPIDERS EAT?

When it's time for dinner, a spider traps its prey before injecting it with a chemical that turns the bug's insides to mush. The spider then sucks out the liquid like a bug milkshake.

DO FEMALE SPIDERS EAT MALES?

The female black widow spider eats the male after mating, sometimes eating up to 25 partners a day. Now that's a real man-eater!

WHAT IS THE WORLD'S HEAVIEST SPIDER?

The record for the world's heaviest spider was a giant bird-eating spider found in Suriname in 1965. It weighed 122 g (4 oz). That's about the same as a large apple!

CAN HUMANS USE SPIDER WEBS?

Eastern European peasants used to make wound dressings out of spiders' webs. Spider silk has antiseptic properties, so it wasn't such a bad idea.

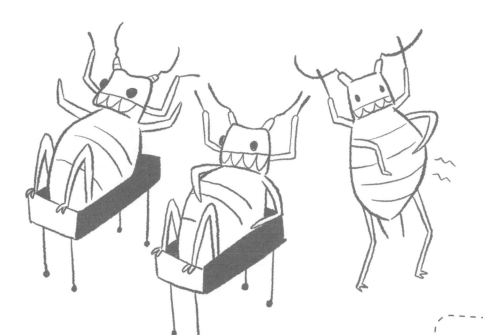

DID YOU KNOW?

Greenfly, or aphids, are actually born pregnant with clones (exact copies of themselves) that they later give birth to. Weird!

HOW MUCH DO CATERPILLARS EAT?

The caterpillar of the polyphemus moth chomps its way through 86,000 times its own birth weight in food in the first 56 days of its life. That would be the same as a human baby munching through about 150,000 burgers!

HOW MUCH BLOOD DOES A LEECH DRINK?

A leech will only finish sucking blood when it is five times its original size. The blood consumed in a single meal can keep a leech alive for up to nine months.

ARE THERE ANY DANGEROUS SNAILS?

Yes, absolutely. The sting of a tropical cone snail can be fatal to a human being. Luckily, they live underwater, so you should be safe in your garden.

DID YOU KNOW?

A scorpion can withstand up to 200 times the amount of radiation that would kill a human.

WHICH SCORPION IS THE DEADLIEST TO HUMANS?

The fat-tailed scorpion is responsible for most human deaths from scorpion stings. Although its venom is less toxic than that of the deathstalker scorpion, it injects more into its victim.

HOW DOES THE TONGUE LOUSE FIND FOOD?

The tongue louse is a type of parasite that crawls in through a fish's gills and then chews off the fish's tongue. It spends the rest of its life acting as its victim's tongue while feeding off the blood supply of the fish.

DO TERMITES EXPLODE?

To defend their territory, guard termites sometimes make themselves explode to scare off attackers.

HOW FAR DOES A BEE FLY TO COLLECT NECTAR FOR HONEY?

A honeybee travels an average of 1,60 round trips in order to produce six teaspoons of honey. To produce 1 kg (2.2 lb) of honey, a bee has to travel a distance equal to four times around the Earth.

CAN YOU EAT TERMITES?

In South Africa, termites are roasted and eaten as snacks, just like popcorn.

DO BABY BIRDS POOP IN THEIR NEST?

Yes. The great tit produces its feces in tiny sacs that it later removes from its nest. The average tit removes around 500 of these sacs from its nest each week— that's one busy little pooper!

ARE SQUIRRELS DANGEROUS?

A pine-cone shortage in eastern Russia drove a gang of ravenous squirrels to attack and eat a stray dog.

HOW FAR CAN STINKBUGS SPIT?

Some stinkbugs are able to spit their smelly goo as far as 30 cm (1 ft). Not bad for a bug often no more than 1.5 cm (half an inch) long!

CAN WHALES EXPLODE?

A decomposing sperm whale exploded in Taiwan in 2004 as it was being transported for a post-mortem. Nearby shops and cars were showered with blood, guts, and blubber. A build-up of natural gases inside the whale was to blame.

DOES ANY CREATURE EAT HAIR?

The giant cricket of Africa enjoys eating human hair. Nobody knows why!

HOW BIG IS A SINGLE ELEPHANT POOP?

An elephant can produce a 38 kg (83 lb) pile of poop in one go. An elephant produces around 150 kg (330 lb) of dung every day.

HOW DO YOU CURE A POLAR BEAR'S BAD BREATH?

Vets at Seneca Park Zoo, USA, had to use a hammer and chisel to remove an infected tooth from a polar bear in 2005. The tooth had been giving the bear bad breath. How they got close enough to find out is a mystery!

HOW DOES A HIPPO MARK ITS TERRITORY?

To mark its territory, a hippopotamus spins its tail while pooping, as the spinning helps spread the stinky stuff around.

WHAT'S IN BIRD'S NEST SOUP?

Cave swiftlets of Southeast Asia make nests from their own saliva. Locals use the dried nests to make the delicacy bird's nest soup—yes, it's a soup made from spit!

WHAT CREATURE LIKES SMELLY FEET?

Mosquitoes love stinky human feet because of the enzymes found on them.

WHICH ANIMAL HAS ATTRACTIVE FARTS?

The fart of a female southern pine beetle contains a pheromone called frontalin, which attracts male beetles.

WHICH ANIMAL PEES AND EATS AT THE SAME TIME?

Vampire bats urinate the whole time that they're sucking blood. This ensures they don't get so full of blood that they're too heavy to fly.

BRILLIANT BODIES

WHY DO WE NEED SKIN AND HAIR?

Your "outer wrappings" of skin, hair, teeth, and nails do a lot more than keep up appearances. Between them, they protect you from damage or infection and keep you at the right temperature. Your skin acts as a blanket against the cold and allows heat to escape when you're hot.

ARE WE REALLY COVERED IN DEAD SKIN?

The skin that you see is made up of dead skin cells. New cells are constantly forming at the base of the epidermis. They then begin the journey upward. Older cells, nearer the surface, die and rise to the surface as these new cells replace them.

DID YOU KNOW?

Your skin is the largest of the body's organs. Laid flat, a 13-year-old's skin would cover around 1.7 m^2 (18 square feet)—about the size of a single bed.

HOW DOES SKIN WORK?

It is divided into layers. The bit that you can see, called the epidermis, is the outside layer. It forms the protective barrier for your body. The layer beneath is the dermis, which contains blood vessels, sweat glands, and hair follicles. The bottom layer, called the hypodermis, connects your skin with your muscles.

HOW STRONG IS HAIR?

An object of around 100 g (3 oz) could dangle on a single strand of human hair. That's nearly two regular-sized bars of soap! It's not quite as strong as steel, but it's up there with other strong substances like Kevlar, used to make bulletproof vests.

WHAT IS HAIR MADE OF?

Hair is mostly made up of a protein called keratin. It is the same substance that makes your fingernails and toenails. It is also what animals' hooves, claws, horns, and even feathers and beaks are made of. It's useful stuff!

WHY DON'T WOMEN HAVE BEARDS?

Facial hair was common in our ancestors, but now it's absent in most women. The difference seems to be down to evolution. Humans have become less hairy in the millions of years since we developed from apes. Over time, men came to prefer women with little or no facial hair. Those women would pass on this "hairless" gene to their daughters. Then those girls would have a head start in the ancient dating game.

HOW LONG IS THE LONGEST BEARD?

The longest beard ever measured stretched out to 5.33 m (17½ feet).

WHY AREN'T THE PALMS OF OUR HANDS HAIRY?

Even the furriest, hairiest mammals have no hair follicles on the palms of their hands or soles of their feet. Hairs would be worn away by the constant contact with the ground, and this would make it more difficult to grip onto things.

WHY DON'T WOMEN GO BALD?

Women may not have beards, but they usually keep the hair on the top of their head all their life. For the same reason that men have beards, it's down to hormones. The male hormone testosterone can make hair follicles shrivel up until no more hair grows. Although women produce some testosterone, their female hormones protect their hair.

WHY DO WE GROW TWO SETS OF TEETH?

It might seem odd replacing a full set of teeth, but your first set of milk (or baby) teeth has done its job by the time you're five or six years old. They've helped you chew and get important nourishment, as well as learn to talk. It's time for your body to prepare to house a larger, adult set of teeth.

ARE ADULT TEETH TOUGHER THAN BABY TEETH?

No, they're just bigger! Your 20 milk teeth do their job very well, allowing you to slice, cut, and grind food. But you need more teeth to fill your larger, adult jaw. The first set helps your jaw grow in a way that will let your second set replace that first set—and still have room for the 12 extra teeth that adults have.

WHAT MAKES TEETH SO STRONG?

The outer layer of your teeth is covered in enamel, the hardest tissue in your body.

WHAT IS AN INFECTION?

Micro-organisms are the tiny, invisible germs all around us. Some of these bacteria and viruses are safe or even helpful. But harmful micro-organisms can enter the body, where they multiply quickly and cause illnesses. Such an invasion is called an infection.

WHY DON'T HUMANS HAVE CLAWS?

Most mammals have sharp claws to help them dig or to attack other animals. Primates, the group of mammals that includes monkeys, apes, and humans, have nails instead. As primates developed, claws became smaller and flatter. These smaller versions, nails, are better for handling small objects, such as nuts and fruit, and working with tools—something that other mammals rarely do.

IS IT BAD TO BITE YOUR NAILS?

Chewing on dirty nails can introduce germs into your body and lead to infections if you damage the skin.

HAVE PEOPLE ALWAYS WASHED?

Yes, even in ancient history. So, you have no excuse for soap dodging! Ancient Rome's Baths of Caracalla could hold 1,600 bathers at the same time.

WHAT IF YOUR HANDS LOOK CLEAN?

It's important to wash your hands regularly, and especially before you eat. Because germs are small enough to be invisible, you might think that your hands are completely clean. But your hands are constantly touching other things—doorknobs, books, or other people's hands—and that contact transmits germs.

WHY DO I HAVE TO SHOWER?

Your body has many ways of fighting back against illness and infection. But we can do a lot to help it fight off bacteria and viruses. Sensible cleaning habits, known as hygiene, can remove those harmful germs—which are too small for us to see.

HOW DO OUR BONES TELL A STORY?

Most parts of a body decompose (break down) after a person dies. Bones take much longer to decompose and can even become fossils, so they can tell us about our ancestors many thousands or even millions of years ago. Scientists can tell how humans have changed and what type of injuries and illnesses ancient humans faced.

WHAT WOULD WE BE LIKE WITHOUT BONES?

Every building needs protection on the outside and strong supports running through it to stop it from toppling over. Your body is just the same. Without the support provided by your bones, you'd flop over like a rag doll. The framework of bones is called the skeleton.

WHAT DOES YOUR SKELETON PROTECT?

Your body contains many delicate organs such as the heart, lungs, and brain. It hurts even if your tough outer layers get bumped. Things would be much worse if your skeleton didn't protect your sensitive internal organs.

HOW MANY BONES ARE THERE IN YOUR BODY?

A human adult skeleton contains 206 bones. There are several types of bones. Your fingers, toes, arms, and legs contain long bones. Your wrists and feet have short bones for support and stability. Flat bones, including your hips, ribs, and shoulder blades, are strong for protecting vital organs.

WHAT IS THE SMALLEST BONE IN THE BODY?

The smallest bone is the 2.8 mm (0.11 in) stirrup bone, which is found in the ear.

CAN WE CHANGE OUR BONES?

Eating the right foods helps to make your bones strong and hard. Exercise also strengthens bones. Over time, the bones of athletes become tougher and thicker. Bones in the arm a tennis player uses regularly are often larger than in their other arm.

Hello?

HOW DO BONES HELP US TO HEAR?

Tiny bones inside your ear carry sound vibrations to your brain, where they are converted into information about what you heard.

CAN BONES BEND?

Bones are flexible, so they don't snap in half at the first sign of stress. However, they don't bend very much. Instead, we move our body into different positions using the connections between bones. Your skeleton is helped by joints, muscles, tendons, and ligaments.

WHAT'S INSIDE A BONE?

The hard white outside of a bone is called compact bone. Nerves and blood vessels of the periosteum, a thin membrane, nourish this outer layer. The layer of spongy bone inside helps keep your bones flexible. The soft marrow, found inside many bones, is like a factory producing blood cells for the whole body.

95

HOW DO BONES MOVE?

Your bones meet each other at junctions called joints. Some joints, like your knees, work like hinges and let bones swing back and forth. Others, like your shoulders, allow even more movement. In each case, tough tissues called ligaments attach to both bones and act like pulleys.

WHAT HAPPENS IF YOU BREAK A BONE?

Bones, like other parts of your body, are usually able to recover from serious injury. Within minutes of a break, your body starts to heal. It completes its task in stages, first stopping blood from escaping and finishing with a new piece of bone where the break has been.

WHY DO YOU NEED TO HAVE A CAST?

An injured bone can be knocked out of place if it is bumped, so a cast acts as a shock absorber. Sometimes, metal pins are inserted to hold a broken bone in place.

CAN BONES GET SICK?

Any part of your body can become injured or diseased. If it happens to your bones, your body can lose mobility and support, as well as some of its ability to produce new blood cells. Some conditions arise because of wear and tear, but infections can also develop quickly.

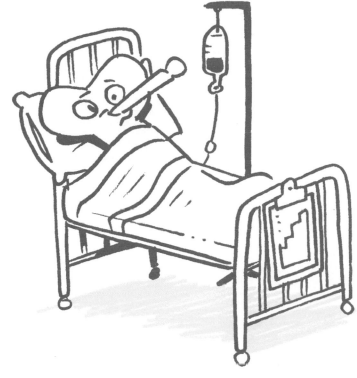

DO PEOPLE SHRINK AS THEY GET OLDER?

As people age, gravity takes its toll on the spine. The discs between the vertebrae get squeezed, so people can look a little bit shorter.

DO OLDER PEOPLE HAVE WEAKER BONES?

Bones are like factories, constantly working. They produce blood cells all the time, but as people get older, some of the work slows down. Bone-building cells, which constantly renew bones, often can't keep bones as strong. Bones become less dense and weaker as a result.

WHEN ARE BONES STRONGEST?

Young bones get stronger as part of the growing process, especially if you eat well and exercise. They are strongest in your twenties. After that, bone strength decreases unless you exercise regularly.

CAN BONES BE FAT?

Your bones can't grow fatter, but they do store fat inside. Bones hold emergency supplies of energy, stored as fat in yellow bone marrow. They also store vital minerals that your body needs to function, and the blood cells they produce help you stay healthy and recover from injury.

WHAT IS A TRANSPLANT?

In a healthy person, bone marrow produces cells for the whole body. Some health conditions prevent this from happening properly. Healthy cells from one person's marrow can be transplanted into a sick person's body to help their marrow work better. Blood can also be taken from one person and given to another person if they need it.

WHY DO WE NEED MUSCLES?

We need muscles to perform just about any activity that involves movement. These bundles of fibrous (stringy) tissues do so many things. They move your bones, open your eyes, and help you chew. Many of them work automatically, pumping your heart, helping you digest food, and making sure you breathe regularly.

HOW DO HELMETS PROTECT YOUR SKULL?

Protective clothing and pads shield people from forces that could injure or break bones. Bike helmets help to protect your skull and your brain. Their hard outer layer spreads the force of an impact from one area. The softer, inner layer absorbs that force, so that less of it reaches your head.

WHY CAN YOU HEAR YOUR HEART?

Each thump of your heartbeat is the sound of a heart muscle forcing a heart valve (part of the heart that controls the flow of blood) shut.

WHAT DO MUSCLES LOOK LIKE?

If you looked closely at an elastic band, you'd see that it is made up of strands that stretch and then tighten up again. Close up, muscles look a lot like that, but they have special shapes to match their job. All of them respond to signals from your brain, telling them to contract (tighten) or relax.

HOW MANY MUSCLES ARE THERE IN YOUR BODY?

Your body has about 640 muscles. Some people consider some of those to be groups of smaller muscles, so the total could be much higher. Whatever the number, they make up three main groups: Skeletal (which move bones), cardiac (in your heart), and smooth (mainly in your digestive system).

HOW BIG IS YOUR HEART?

Lock your hands together with the fingers entwined. That's about the size of your heart.

HOW DO MUSCLES HELP US MOVE?

Skeletal muscles help you move around. They are connected to bones with tough tissues called tendons and work by pulling rather than pushing. As a muscle contracts, it pulls a tendon connected to a bone. That pulls the bone with it. You're in control of these muscles, which tighten or relax as you instruct them.

WHY DO MUSCLES WORK IN PAIRS?

Muscles often pair up on each side of a bone or joint. When you bend your arm, you're tightening the biceps muscle on one side of your upper arm. At the same time, you're relaxing the triceps muscle underneath. To straighten out again, you just do the opposite with the pair.

DO DIFFERENT PEOPLE HAVE DIFFERENT MUSCLES?

We all have the same number of muscles, but their shapes and sizes differ. That gives some people a head start in certain activities, such as long-distance running or swimming.

CAN MUSCLES REALLY REMEMBER?

It's true that muscles can seem to remember a series of movements in the right order. It's called muscle memory. But in reality, it's your brain that's calling the shots. Like a computer with a set of stored commands, your brain stores a series of signals that it sends out to muscles when certain actions are needed.

CAN MUSCLE MEMORY HELP YOU PLAY THE PIANO?

Yes, but it's not a question of how big your muscles are, but how many times you've used them to play a sequence of notes.

CAN WE EXERCISE TOO MUCH?

Feeling the burn is a sign that your muscles have been working hard. That can be a good thing, but it's also one of the signals that things have gone too far and that you need rest. If too much lactic acid is left behind, then your muscles can be damaged.

CAN YOUR MUSCLES TURN YOU INTO A CAVEMAN?

When you're suddenly scared, your brain sends a signal to glands that produce a chemical called epinephrine (or adrenaline). Your heart rate speeds up and blood rushes to your muscles, ready for you to fight anything dangerous or run away from it, just as early humans once would have done when under attack.

CAN HEART MUSCLES MIX UP SIGNALS?

Yes, they can. Some people can have an irregular heartbeat treated with a device called a pacemaker, which sends out regular pulses to the cardiac muscles.

HOW DOES YOUR HEART KEEP IN RHYTHM?

The outer walls of your heart contain a group of muscle cells that produces a small electrical current. These electrical pulses make your heart beat at a safe, steady pace.

103

HOW DO MUSCLES BUILD UP?

If you and a weight lifter stood next to each other and flexed your muscles, the weight lifter's muscles would look much bigger than yours. Weight lifters build up their muscles by lifting heavy loads. But it's more important that you keep your muscles strong with regular exercise than focus on bodybuilding!

WHAT IS A MUSCLE CRAMP?

Chemicals are exchanged each time muscles contract and relax. The tissues in a resting muscle are long and stretched. When the tissues tighten and the muscle contracts, calcium rushes in and sodium (salt) goes out. Normally, the muscle relaxes again quickly, but sometimes it stays tightly and painfully constricted. That's a muscle cramp.

DOES EXERCISE AFTER EATING CAUSE CRAMPS?

Probably not, but you are likely to feel sick or sluggish if you exercise too soon after eating. During exercise, your blood flow is diverted to your muscles from your digestive system. This can make it harder to deal with large amounts of food.

DO MUSCLES NEED SPECIAL FUEL?

Muscles get most of their energy from glucose, a type of sugar that is found in many foods. They use oxygen contained in the blood to convert the glucose into energy. This is a chemical reaction, and it also releases water and carbon dioxide. The energy can be used immediately or stored as fuel for later.

WHAT HAPPENS WHEN WE SHIVER?

Your body can sense when cold is a threat. The brain sends signals to muscles on your skin, making them contract and relax very quickly. As they do so, they release heat.

WHY DO TENNIS PLAYERS EAT BANANAS?

Bananas contain lots of carbohydrates (which release glucose) as well as potassium, which helps prevent muscle cramps.

WHY DOES HARD EXERCISE "BURN" SOMETIMES?

Have you heard people talk about "feeling the burn" when their muscles are working hard? That's because oxygen in your blood helps your muscles use glucose to produce energy. If you're exercising really hard, then the muscles use up all the oxygen in the blood nearby. The muscles now start to turn sugar into oxygen. Lactic acid is left behind, giving your muscles a burning feeling.

WHAT CAUSES GOOSE BUMPS?

Muscles cause tiny hairs on your body to stand up, pulling skin up in bumps. The standing hairs trap warm air to act as a blanket against the cold. The scientific name is horripilation!

DO OLDER PEOPLE NEED TO EXERCISE?

Some muscle turns to fat as people get older, so it's important to exercise regularly to keep those muscle levels maintained.

WHAT ARE ORGANS?

Animal or plant cells with a similar function can group together to form living tissue. Each tissue does a particular job, such as taking up water (in plants) or lining your intestine to help food move smoothly on its way.

Different tissues combine to form the organs of the body, which carry out their own particular jobs inside you. Your heart, for example, contains fibrous tissue, muscle tissue, and other special cells to control how it beats. These organs can be grouped together in systems. Some items on the list of organs might surprise you: Your tongue, for instance, is an organ that helps you talk, chew, taste, and swallow.

DID YOU KNOW?

Your eye is an organ! It is an organ that reacts to light to allow you to see. It is less developed in babies; they only see black and white to begin with.

HOW MANY ORGANS DO WE HAVE?

Different people count in different ways. We have five vital organs: The brain, lungs, heart, liver, and kidneys, and around 70 others.

WHY DOES YOUR BRAIN TAKE CONTROL OF YOUR BODY?

Keep thinking of your body as being like a team. To be effective, the players (human organs) need to work together. They follow the orders of the coach, who has an overview of everything. Your brain is like a coach, constantly observing what's happening and sending out orders to the rest of the body.

IS THERE SUCH A THING AS "BRAIN FOOD"?

Certain foods are good for your brain. Fish, nuts, broccoli, avocado, and—wait for it—small amounts of dark chocolate can improve memory, learning, and concentration skills.

WHAT CAN WE TRAIN OUR BRAIN TO DO?

We train our brain when we learn new skills and actions: Reading, playing the guitar, or skiing. The brain stores the instructions for later use. These are called conscious activities because we control them. At the same time, the brain does many important jobs automatically. Luckily, we can't untrain our brain to signal how to breathe or digest food.

WHY DOES BLOOD LOOK RED?

The blood moving around your body contains varying amounts of oxygen. This reacts with an iron-rich protein in your red blood cells, turning it red—just as iron turns rusty red when it meets oxygen in the air. Blood with lots of oxygen is bright red, and gets darker as it releases the oxygen around the body. Some creatures, such as spiders and lobsters, have copper instead of iron in their blood, making it blue.

HOW MUCH BLOOD DOES YOUR HEART PUMP?

An adult body has at least 4 l (1 gallon) of blood, which carries essential chemicals to every part of the body, so that muscles and organs work properly. The blood completes the return journey from those parts, carrying waste. In order to move this amount of blood all the time, you need a strong, reliable pump—your heart.

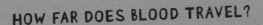

HOW FAR DOES BLOOD TRAVEL?

The human body contains 96,000 km (60,000 miles) of blood vessels. Blood cells travel along these highways and byways many times every day!

WHY IS IT HARD TO HOLD YOUR BREATH?

It starts to hurt if you try to hold your breath for too long. That's your brain telling you to let your lungs do their work. It's their job to get the oxygen from each breath in, and get rid of carbon dioxide and other wastes when you exhale. You need your lungs to provide the breath for moving, speaking, singing, and laughing.

HOW LONG CAN SOME PEOPLE HOLD THEIR BREATH?

Some deep-sea divers can hold their breath for more than 20 minutes, but most people can manage only a minute.

DO YOUR LUNGS HAVE MUSCLES?

Your lungs can't breathe without help. And that help comes from a big muscle beneath them, called the diaphragm. When it tightens, air rushes into your chest (and lungs). Relaxing it reduces the space in your chest, forcing you to breathe out.

IS YAWNING CATCHING?

Yes, it is, but no one is quite sure why. Human beings and chimpanzees are the only animals that yawn when they see each other yawn. But it gets even stranger. Very small children don't yawn when someone near them does. As they get older, people seem to learn to do copycat yawning. So a single yawn can set a whole roomful of people off!

HOW FAST IS THE AIR IN A SNEEZE?

Air rushes out of your nose and mouth at more than 160 km/h (100 mph) when you sneeze. It's one of your body's ways of keeping your nose clear. Usually, you have no control over whether you're going to sneeze. That's because it is a natural reflex and not something you can plan. A typical sneeze contains up to 40,000 tiny drops of liquid mixed in with the air.

HOW LOUD IS THE LOUDEST BURP?

A burp is a harmless way of getting rid of air or gas that you might have swallowed. Carbonated drinks often make you burp because they are full of gas. Normally, you can control how the gas will be released, so you can keep things pretty quiet. The world record for the loudest burp is 107 decibels. That's as loud as a lawn mower running next to you.

DID YOU KNOW?

It takes the stomach about three to four hours to break solid food down into a liquidy mush called chyme. The chyme is then sent on to the intestines.

HOW BIG IS YOUR STOMACH?

Well, it depends on your body size! The organ that is called the stomach is the size of a fist, but it doesn't take up the whole of your "tummy" space. The other parts of your digestive system sit in that space, too. The first stop is the stomach, then food moves on through the intestines.

HOW MUCH CAN YOUR STOMACH STRETCH?

Your stomach is shaped like a letter J and has three main jobs: Storing food, turning the food into more of a liquid, and sending it on to the small intestine. It needs to be stretchy for that first job, and your stomach can extend to 20 times its resting size after a big meal.

WHY DOES YOUR TUMMY RUMBLE SOMETIMES?

Stomach muscles constantly squeeze food to break it up. Sometimes gases and air are squeezed out of the food ... and rumble inside.

WHY DO WE THROW UP?

Nausea—the sick feeling before you throw up—is a signal that your body needs to get rid of something harmful. Throwing up isn't nice, but you often feel better afterward, proving that it was necessary. Feeling sick is your body's way of giving you a message, just like an ache or pain stops you from using tired or damaged muscles.

WHY IS POOP BROWN?

The liver produces a chemical called bile that helps digest fats. Extra bile is stored in an organ called the gall bladder. When bile reacts with bacteria in your gut, it turns the waste brown.

WHAT DO WE MEAN BY RICH FOOD?

Rich food isn't food for rich people. It is food high in fats, such as butter and cream, which take longer to digest.

HOW BIG IS THE LIVER?

It is the largest internal organ in the body, weighing about 1.4 kg (3 lb). It grows as you do, reaching full size by about age 15: Around 15 cm (6 in) across. With more than 500 tasks to perform, from digesting food and breaking down toxins, to helping the blood clot, it's not surprising that the liver is so big.

WHAT IS THE LIVER'S MOST IMPORTANT JOB?

If you asked ten specialist doctors, you might get ten different answers, because the liver does so much. But the really vital job— sometimes needed to save your life—is to clean the poisons in your system. That's the liver's "emergency department" role, although the other 499 (or more) jobs are important.

WHICH IS YOUR BUSIEST ORGAN?

Your liver performs hundreds of jobs to keep your body working. You absolutely could not live without it—and it is so special that part of a liver can regrow into a whole one. The liver processes your food, stores the energy, gets rid of waste, and cleans your blood, as well as hundreds of other important tasks.

WHAT ARE YOUR KIDNEYS FOR?

Your two fist-sized kidneys, located near the middle of your back, filter your blood to remove waste material and excess water. About 200 l (50 gallons) of blood passes through them each day. The blood comes out cleaner, and the waste and water gets sent off as urine.

WHY ARE WE SO FULL OF WASTE?

Your blood delivers nutrients around your body. Sometimes it brings stuff you already have enough of. Other stuff is broken down by chemical reactions in your cells, which can produce waste products— a bit like a car exhaust. Water leaves your body as sweat, in your breath, and also in your poop, but the majority of it goes into your urine.

HOW DO YOU KNOW WHEN YOU NEED TO PEE?

Urine gathers in an organ called the bladder. When it gets full, the bladder sends a message to your brain that it is emptying-out time!

WHAT IF YOUR KIDNEYS DON'T WORK?

You could get by with one kidney if the other becomes damaged. But losing a second kidney would cause serious problems because of the build-up of waste in your blood. Dialysis machines can take the place of kidneys, filtering blood and returning it to the patient's body.

WHAT IS YOUR APPENDIX FOR?

The appendix is a small tube attached to your large intestine. That's where your body digests food, except the human appendix doesn't seem to digest anything. Many scientists believe that it once helped human ancestors—today's apes—to digest leaves and twigs.

DO YOU REALLY HAVE A TAIL?

If you look behind any of your friends, you won't see any tail. But every human does have a tail bone, called the coccyx, at the base of the back. It's all that's left of a tail that our ancestors had millions of years ago—just as monkeys still have.

DO SOME ORGANS JUST DO NOTHING?

It might seem strange to think that your body carries around excess baggage that serves no purpose. But some parts of your body do seem to be souvenirs of a time when your ancestors—long ago—needed them to survive in very different conditions. Over time, these body parts get smaller, but some never go away.

WHY ARE CELLS DIFFERENT SHAPES?

Cells are different shapes to help them perform different tasks. Red blood cells, for example, are shaped like donuts as it's the best way to float in your blood where they carry oxygen. Nerve cells have long sections that look like tiny wires—ideal for carrying electrical signals to your brain and other parts of your body.

WHAT DO CELLS DO?

They carry out special jobs like providing energy, fighting attackers, carrying away waste, and much more. Groups of similar cells teaming up are called tissue. Lots of tissue working together is known as an organ and the biggest collection of cells— working all over your body in different networks— becomes known as a system.

HOW MANY CELLS ARE IN YOUR BODY?

Humans, like other living things, are made up of collections of cells. They are the building blocks of your body, able to grow and reproduce. These cells group together to become the systems that oversee all the work for the body to stay healthy. It's hard to judge how many there are, but scientists' recent estimates come in at around 37 trillion!

WHAT ARE YOUR BODY'S "SYSTEMS?"

There are at least ten systems performing the jobs in your body that make you work so well. Here are some of them:

- the circulatory system, which carries blood around your body

- the nervous system, which carries messages and sends signals

- the skeletal system, which supports, protects, and moves you around

- the respiratory system, which brings in air and removes carbon dioxide

- the muscular system, which helps you move, breathe, and function

- the digestive system, which breaks down food and removes waste

IS YOUR SKIN AN ORGAN OR A SYSTEM?

The answer is ... both! It's the body's largest organ, but the way that it combines fighting disease, storing fat, and getting rid of waste makes it a system as well.

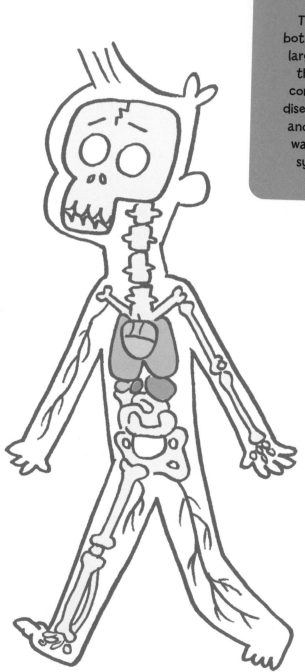

DOES RESTING HELP YOUR BODY'S SYSTEMS?

Regular rest, or taking time off after exercise, helps your systems maintain their strength.

HOW DID YOU START OUT?

The tiniest amount of material from your mother and father combined to set things under way to produce something special— you. Contained inside that material was all the information your body would need to become a human being.

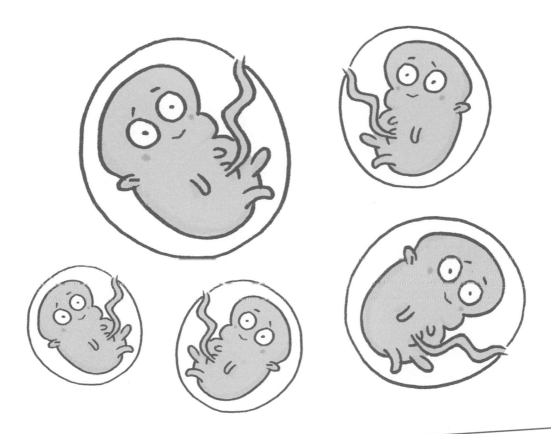

DO WE REALLY START OUT AS TWO CELLS?

A sperm cell from your father combined with (or fertilized) an egg cell inside your mother. The sperm had competition from hundreds of millions of other sperm cells, each trying to reach the single egg cell. Women usually produce just one egg cell each month.

HOW LONG DO WE LIVE INSIDE OUR MOTHER?

The period from that first meeting of sperm and egg cells all the way to the birth of a baby is called gestation. It normally takes about 40 weeks. During that time, we develop and grow, so that we're able to eat and breathe as soon as we are born.

WHAT EXACTLY IS BLOOD?

Your blood is a combination of red cells (to carry oxygen), white cells (to fight infection), platelets (to stop bleeding), and a yellowish liquid called plasma. In addition to feeding and protecting your body, blood can cool you down by sending heat to your skin when you're too warm inside. That's why many people look red-faced when they're hot.

HOW DOES BLOOD TRAVEL?

Your blood travels along a network of large and small channels called blood vessels. It goes out from the heart and lungs along arteries and returns along veins to be refreshed. This out-and-back movement is called circulating, so your blood is part of your circulatory system.

WHAT CAUSES A BRUISE?

A bump to your body can cause tiny blood vessels to break. Blood leaks out of the broken vessels and fills part of the area. Damaged blood cells flow toward the surface of the skin, showing up as a bruise around the injured area.

HOW FAST DOES BLOOD TRAVEL?

It takes just about a minute for blood to make the journey from your heart, around your body, and back to your heart again.

HOW DOES YOUR BRAIN MAKE SENSE OF INFORMATION?

The central nervous system consists of the brain and the spinal cord (inside the backbone). Incoming information is processed in special areas concentrating on sound, sight, movement, and so on. Sensory nerves send impulses to the brain, and motor nerves send signals out.

HOW DOES YOUR BODY CARRY MESSAGES?

Your body needs a network to send messages back and forth—calling for more blood or for help to fight infection, or just to pass on how good a pizza smells. The nervous system does that job, relaying signals up to the brain and out to everywhere in your body.

ARE YOUR NERVES FULL OF ELECTRICITY?

The nervous system links billions of nerve cells, or neurons, in a series of paths leading to and from your brain. The signals that travel along this network are called impulses. The impulses combine electricity and chemistry to jump from one neuron to the next along the way. The gap between neurons is called a synapse.

DO ALL LIVING THINGS BREATHE?

Animals and plants both need certain gases to live and must get rid of other harmful gases. Even bacteria use respiration to stay alive. Plants must take in carbon dioxide and "breathe out" oxygen. We do the opposite—inhaling to get oxygen and exhaling to get rid of carbon dioxide and other wastes.

HOW DO MUSCLES GET OXYGEN?

Oxygen is transported through your circulatory system in red blood cells. Muscles need oxygen just as a fire needs air: To burn things. Your muscles use oxygen to burn sugars and fats in order to release energy through chemical reactions.

WHAT IS A VOICE BOX?

It's the scientific term for the larynx, which has tissue folds (vocal cords) that vibrate to make sounds when air passes through.

DID YOU KNOW?

Not all bacteria is bad. More than 500 different types of bacteria help your body digest food, get rid of waste ... and kill bad bacteria.

HOW DOES YOUR BODY FIGHT DISEASE?

Your immune system is able to call on most other systems to do something very important—keep you healthy by defending against viruses, bacteria, and parasites. It can identify a problem, find the right weapons for a battle, and make sure that you're prepared next time you face that threat.

SHOULD YOU REALLY "STARVE A FEVER?"

Yes. If you eat, kick-starting your digestive system into action, it will give your body extra work when it really needs to focus on other tasks.

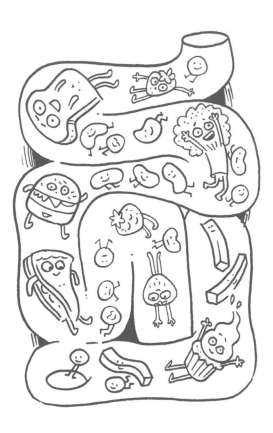

WHAT HAPPENS TO THE FOOD WE EAT?

You might want to eat ice cream and chocolates all day, but your body needs different types of fuel to operate as it should. It relies on the digestive system to turn roast beef, broccoli, spaghetti, and cupcakes— in other words, food—into fuel for your body.

WHY ARE YOUR INTESTINES SO LONG?

Your small intestine (which is longer but skinnier than your large intestine) absorbs nutrients from food as it passes along the way. Its length—about 6 m (20 ft) if uncoiled—gives it lots of surface area to capture food. That surface area is increased further with lots of finger-like shapes called villi.

HOW LONG DOES IT TAKE TO DIGEST A BIG MEAL?

From the time you finish your meal until the last bit of goodness has been extracted can take up to eight hours to pass from the stomach, through the small intestine, and into the large intestine, where the last water is removed and what's left is sent off as waste.

DOES YOUR BRAIN WORK LIKE A COMPUTER?

In many ways, your brain is like a computer, constantly analyzing data and acting on that stimulation. But even the most advanced computer can't match the brain in quickly sending information back along its own system. The most powerful computer is still 30 times slower than your brain!

DO WE NOTICE EVERYTHING AROUND US?

We often focus on one thing and ignore other activities. It's called selective attention. In one experiment, scientists ask viewers to count how often a group of basketball players pass the ball in a short video clip. People concentrate on counting, but they often miss the man in a gorilla costume that walks through the group of players!

DOES YOUR BRAIN NEED EXERCISE?

Yes! Doctors recommend reading, playing musical instruments, and doing puzzles as ways of keeping the brain "fit" well into old age.

WHAT HAPPENS WHEN WE SEE DOUBLE?

If your eyes aren't looking in exactly the same direction, your brain can't form a single 3-D image so you see two images.

CAN YOU REALLY TASTE WITH YOUR NOSE?

Does your mouth water when you smell lasagna cooking in the oven? And do you find that you can't taste food when your head is blocked up with a cold? These are examples of how your nose and mouth act as a team to guide your sense of taste.

IS A HEADACHE REALLY A PAIN IN YOUR BRAIN?

No. The brain has very few pain receptors, so it can't send out pain signals. Most headaches are caused by pain in muscles in your head and neck.

HOW CAN RUNNING MAKE YOU HAPPY?

Our bodies constantly produce chemicals called hormones that send messages to the rest of our body. Some of these hormones help us fight disease, and others affect our moods. We can become excited, sad, or happy. Exercise releases some positive hormones that can brighten our mood, which is why people sometimes talk about a "runner's high."

WHY DO DOGS VISIT HOSPITALS?

Hospital patients feel happier, but also recover faster, if they have a chance to pat a dog or another pet.

DO WE REALLY HAVE A FUNNY BONE?

What we call the funny bone—that part of your elbow that gives a zinging feeling when you bang it—is actually a nerve rubbing against a bone in your arm.

SPECTACULAR SPACE

WHO WAS THE FIRST HUMAN IN SPACE?

The first human being in space was Russian Yuri Gagarin on April 12, 1961. He spent just 89 minutes in space as pilot of the Soviet spacecraft Vostok 1.

WHAT DID GAGARIN'S MOTHER THINK?

Gagarin didn't tell his mother he was going because the mission was top secret. And he told his wife a later date for the flight (by which time he was home). Just in case, he left her a letter saying he didn't expect to return and she should remarry if he died.

WHAT DID SPUTNIK DO?

Sputnik whizzed around in Earth orbit at 28,800 km/h (17,900 mph). It made 1,440 orbits, each taking just 96.2 minutes, before burning up re-entering Earth's atmosphere on January 4, 1958.

CAN WE HEAR SOUNDS FROM OTHER PLANETS?

A rover that landed on Mars in 2021 has two microphones, which meant it could send back to Earth the sounds of its own landing and can now record the sound of travel across the surface of the planet. We can hear its metal wheels crunching over Martian stones.

WHO WAS THE FIRST WOMAN IN SPACE?

Russian cosmonaut Valentina Tereshkova became the first woman in space in 1963, with a three-day trip on Vostok 6. Tereshkova's mother found out when she saw the latest pictures from space on television. She knew her daughter had taken parachute training—but that's all!

IS THERE MUSIC IN SPACE?

The first music broadcast from another planet was a song by the US singer and rapper will.i.am of the Black Eyed Peas. NASA's Curiosity rover broadcast the song back to Earth, but didn't take speakers—so if there is any life on Mars, it didn't get to hear it.

WHAT WILL HAPPEN TO BOTH VOYAGERS?

The Voyagers' instruments will send back data to Earth until around 2030, when their power supplies will fail. The Voyagers will continue going at 48,280 km/h (30,000 mph) forever unless they are destroyed in a collision.

HAS ANY SPACECRAFT LEFT THE SOLAR SYSTEM?

A robotic probe named Voyager 1 is the only spacecraft that has gone beyond the solar system—but Voyager 2 is on the way out, too. Both Voyagers were launched in 1977. Voyager 1 is now 21 billion km (13 billion miles) away. Voyager 1 is so far from the Sun that it takes 18 hours for sunlight to reach it. The spacecraft travels at 17 km (11 miles) per second.

CAN YOU DRINK COFFEE IN SPACE?

In zero gravity, in a spaceship, liquids don't stay where they are. Coffee crawls out of its cup or bottle and floats around in the air.

WHY CAN'T YOU GO TO MARS IN A STRAIGHT LINE?

When spacecraft go to Mars, they loop around the Sun in a curved path. Earth and Mars orbit the Sun at different speeds. The best time to leave is calculated from the positions and speeds of both planets. Mars must be in the right place when the spacecraft's orbit intersects the orbit of Mars.

IS IT SAME FOR THE RETURN JOURNEY?

Astronauts couldn't just do their thing on Mars and then leave. They'd have to wait months for the planets to be in the right place for the return journey.

HAVE METEORITES EVER HIT EARTH?

There are around 190 craters around the world that were created by fallen meteorites. The largest one is in South Africa—it measures more than 190 km (118 miles) in diameter and was created about 2 billion years ago.

HAVE WE TURNED SPACE INTO A DUMP?

Lots of old spacecraft are stuck in orbit around the Sun. When spacecraft are sent somewhere and fail to arrive, they don't just disappear—they end up going around the Sun. At least 34,000 bits of space junk are currently going around and around the Sun.

IS THERE A CAR GOING AROUND THE SUN TOO?

Yes. In 2018, American businessman Elon Musk launched a red Tesla Roadster into space as a test load for the new Falcon Heavy rocket. It's "driven" by a dummy in a spacesuit. A plaque on the engine reads "Made on Earth by humans." The car will reach a maximum speed of 21,600 km/h (13,422 mph).

WHY DON'T ASTRONAUTS BURP?

Without gravity, the gases and liquids in an astonaut's digestive system do not separate. So if an astronaut burped, liquid food would also come out of their mouth. Yuck!

CAN WE COLLECT CHUNKS OF ASTEROIDS?

The probe OSIRIS-REx, launched in 2016, reached the asteroid Bennu in 2018 to map its surface for two years. It is blowing puffs of nitrogen gas at the asteroid to dislodge pieces. OSIRIS-REx is trying to catch at least 60 g (2 oz) of material, then bring it back to Earth in 2023.

WHY IS NASA WORKING ON AN "ICEMOLE?"

NASA will send an IceMole probe to look for life in the oceans of Saturn's moon Enceladus. The ocean beneath the frozen surface of this moon is one of the most likely places to find life beyond Earth.

CAN WE MINE ASTEROIDS FOR PRECIOUS METALS?

A company based in California, USA, and Belgium intends to start mining asteroids for valuable metals and minerals. It's designing a spacecraft that will capture asteroids and drag them through space to a space station (not yet built) for processing.

DID YOU KNOW?

If you cry in space, the tears don't fall—they clump together into a big ball that eventually floats away. Eyesight deteriorates, so astronauts who wear glasses often need stronger ones after a few months in space.

ARE THERE SPACE SPIDERS?

NASA sent two golden orb spiders to the International Space Station (ISS) for 45 days in 2011. They were called Gladys and Esmeralda and they became celebrities.

DO YOU GROW TALLER IN SPACE?

Yes. People grow taller in space without gravity dragging them down. Identical twins Scott and Mark Kelly have been studied by NASA: Scott spent a year on the International Space Station (ISS) while Mark stayed on Earth and their health was compared. After a year in space, Scott Kelly grew 5 cm (2 in).

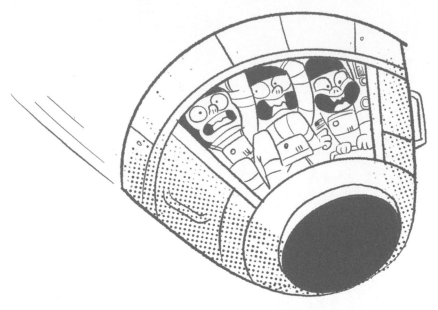

DOES TIME GO AT A DIFFERENT SPEED IN SPACE?

Yes. Astronauts age more slowly than people stuck on Earth, but only very slightly. Time goes more slowly on the International Space Station (ISS) than on Earth. An astronaut on the ISS gains just one hundredth of a second a year.

WHO HAS FLOWN THE FASTEST IN SPACE?

No human has ever flown faster than the crew of Apollo 10. On the way back from orbiting the Moon in 1969, Apollo 10 reached 39,897 km/h (24,791 mph)—the fastest speed ever achieved by a vehicle carrying a crew.

COULD EARTH SPACECRAFT HARM ALIENS?

Every spacecraft carries some microbes from Earth into space. These could contaminate a planet or moon that might have life of its own, possibly causing harm or changing the course of evolution.

WHAT ANIMALS HAVE BEEN INTO SPACE?

Lots of different animals have been into space, including spiders, chicken embryos (in their eggs), newts, jellyfish, bees, and even Mexican jumping beans (there's a worm inside the bean). The first living things sent into space were tiny fruit flies in 1947. They returned safely. A mouse survived going up into space in 1950, but the rocket fell apart coming back and it died.

HAVE ANY MONKEYS BEEN TO SPACE?

The first monkey to reach space was Albert II in 1949, but he died on the return journey. In 1959, two monkeys called Able and Miss Baker survived a 16-minute flight and returned safely.

WHAT ABOUT DOGS?

The most famous animal in space was a Russian stray dog, Laika, in 1957. Sadly, she died on the flight. Also, two Russian dogs, Veterok and Ugolyok, spent 22 days on Kosmos 110 in 1966, setting a record.

WHAT WAS THE FIRST HUMANOID ROBOT IN SPACE?

The first humanoid robot in space was Robonaut 2.0, used on the International Space Station from 2012. Robonaut originally had no legs, but has been given two "climbing manipulators."

CAN ROBOTS HELP US EXPLORE OTHER PLANETS?

NASA's Valkyrie robot will help build on Mars. Valkyrie (or R5) is a humanlike robot, 1.9 m (6 ft 2 in) tall and weighing a hefty 125 kg (275 lb). It can walk, see, use its hands—and put up with terrible working conditions.

WHICH SPACECRAFT SENT THE FIRST DATA FROM ANOTHER PLANET?

In 1970, the Soviet spacecraft Venera 7 arrived at the planet Venus, but it didn't get a soft landing. Its parachute ripped and collapsed on the way through the acidic atmosphere, and Venera slammed into the scorching surface of Venus. It sent back data on its way down, but it then crashed and rolled over so that its antenna was not pointing toward Earth.

WHAT WAS THE FIRST SPACE STATION?

The first space station was Mir, started in 1986. Intended to last five years, it survived 15 years, until 2001. Mir was still going after the country that built it had stopped existing—the USSR broke up in 1991, but Mir lasted another ten years.

WAS THERE A US SPACE STATION?

The United States' only space station, Skylab, was always called an "orbital workshop." Skylab lasted five years, from 1974 to 1979, and had crew for only 171 days of that time. When it fell to Earth, a US newspaper offered a $10,000 prize for finding a piece of it. A 17-year-old Australian claimed it after chunks of the falling Skylab hit his house.

WHO HAS STAYED IN SPACE THE LONGEST?

Cosmonaut Valeri Polyakov holds the record for the longest ever stay in space. He spent nearly 438 days on the space station Mir in a single visit in 1994-1995. That's more than a year and two months.

WHAT CAUSES THE NORTHERN LIGHTS?

The Northern and Southern lights are spectacular displays of swirling, changing shades of green, blue, yellow, red, and violet in the sky. They're made by tiny charged particles streaming from the Sun and colliding with the gases of Earth's atmosphere.

WHERE CAN YOU FIND A REALLY BIG EARTH CRATER?

The Vredefort Crater in South Africa was 380 km (236 miles) across when first created by a massive space rock 2 billion years ago. It's about a third the size of Germany.

DOES EARTH HAVE CRATERS LIKE THE MOON?

Earth is the only rocky planet in the solar system with few craters. Mercury, Mars, and Venus are pitted with huge craters. So is the Moon, but Earth has very few.

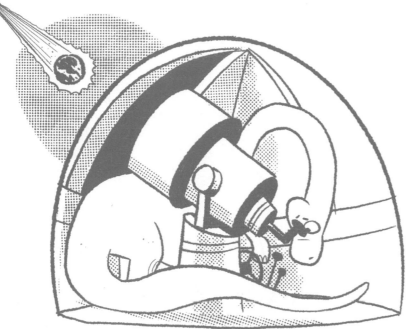

WHAT IF A REALLY BIG ROCK FROM SPACE HIT EARTH?

Space rocks can be deadly. An asteroid that smashed into the Earth about 65 million years ago changed the conditions on the planet so much that many kinds of plants and animals died out, including most dinosaurs.

DO ROCKS FROM SPACE HIT EARTH?

Rocks from space hit Earth all the time. Meteors bombard Earth constantly but, as they whizz through the atmosphere, most get so hot that they burn up completely.

HOW BIG WAS THE ASTEROID THAT HELPED CAUSE THE END OF THE DINOSAURS?

The crater made by the huge space rock was found in the Gulf of Mexico in 1978. The asteroid would have been 15 km (9.3 miles) across.

WHY IS THE EARTH LIKE AN ONION?

Like an onion, the Earth is made up of layers. We live on the crust—the rocks and water that make up the land and seabed. The crust occupies just one hundredth of the volume of the planet. It's about 30 km (18 miles) thick on land and 5 km (3 miles) thick under the oceans.

HAVE EARTH DAYS ALWAYS BEEN 24 HOURS?

No. Days were shorter in the time of the dinosaurs. When Earth first formed, it whizzed round on its axis, four or five times as fast as it does now, and days were just 5-6 hours long, or maybe even shorter.

WHAT'S UNDER EARTH'S CRUST?

Beneath the crust, a thick layer of very hot, molten, semi-liquid rock called magma oozes slowly around the planet. Magma makes up about 84 percent of the planet. Right in the middle, Earth has a super-hot iron core. The outer part of it is molten, and the inner part is a solid ball.

IS THE EARTH ROUND?

Not exactly. The Earth has a fat middle—it's more like a ball that has been squashed from top and bottom, making the middle fatter than it should be and the poles a bit flatter.

SO, WHAT SHAPE IS THE EARTH?

This shape is called an "oblate spheroid," and the chubby piece is called the "equatorial bulge." As the Earth spins on its axis, the forces acting on it push more matter toward the Equator.

DOES THE EARTH HAVE MORE THAN ONE MOON?

Earth has a micro-"moon"—but it only counts as an asteroid. It's called 2016 HO3, which is not a very exciting name for a cosmic companion. It shares Earth's orbit around the Sun and seems to loop around Earth all the time, too.

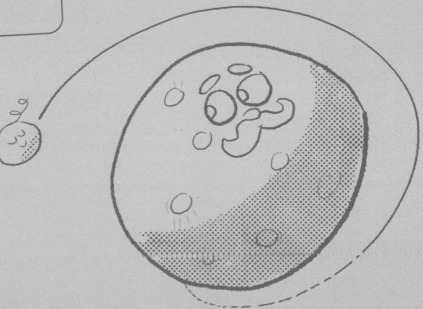

HOW FAST IS THE EARTH SPINNING?

You're moving at over half a million miles an hour. If you stood still at the Equator, Earth's rotation on its axis would mean you'd be moving at 1,600 km/h (1,000 mph). You don't notice it because everything else is moving, too.

DID LIFE ON EARTH EVOLVE FROM ALIENS?

Microbes from outer space could have landed on Earth, and Earth could have had just the right conditions for them to flourish—meaning life on Earth could have evolved from aliens! This theory could explain life in many different star systems. So far, though, we haven't found any microbes on asteroids or comets.

CAN ANY CREATURE SURVIVE IN SPACE WITHOUT A SPACESUIT?

Water bears, or tardigrades, are tiny, tough creatures a fraction of an inch long. They've survived being outside in outer space, where they're freezing cold, bombarded with radiation, and have no oxygen.

HOW HOT IS THE EARTH?

Earth is heated from the inside. The middle of the Earth is really hot—about 6,000°C (10,800°F). The heat comes from the decay of radioactive material and the leftover heat from the time Earth formed, around 4,600 billion years ago.

WHY DOESN'T ALL THE EARTH FREEZE AT NIGHT?

The Earth's atmosphere makes a good blanket, trapping heat close to the surface. Without it, a lot of heat would escape at night and heat would beat down on us during the day (and we'd have nothing to breathe!)

WHY IS EARTH COLDER AT THE POLES?

The rays that bring light and heat from the Sun strike Earth from right above the Equator, but from a lower angle elsewhere in the sky. At the poles, the same amount of sunlight is spread out over a greater area of land, so it has less heating effect.

145

IS THE EARTH A BIG MAGNET?

At the Earth's core, liquid iron is moving around solid iron. This turns the Earth into a magnet, with one magnetic pole near the Geographic North Pole and one near the Geographic South Pole. The magnetic field extends out into space and affects the solar wind (particles streaming from the Sun).

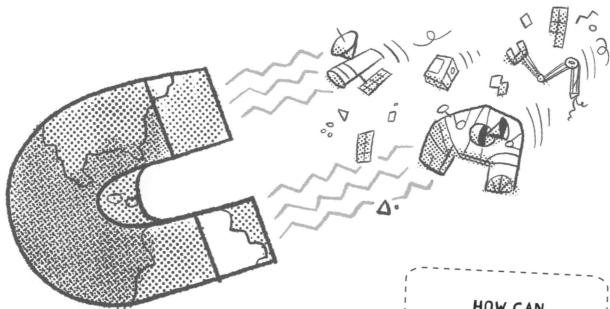

WHICH IS THE NEAREST PLANET TO EARTH?

Earth's nearest planet is Mars—usually. Sometimes it's Venus. They swap around!

HOW CAN PLANETS SWAP POSITION?

Mars, Venus, and Earth all orbit around the Sun at different speeds, which means Mars and Earth are sometimes on opposite sides of the Sun. Venus is on a smaller orbit than Mars because it's closer to the Sun.

IS THERE WEATHER IN SPACE?

You don't just have to worry about rain on Earth—space weather affects the planet, too. The "weather" in space is produced by bursts of energy of different kinds and particles from the Sun.

HOW DOES "SPACE WEATHER" AFFECT EARTH?

Space weather can affect GPS and communications satellites so they don't work properly. It can disrupt the electric power grid that brings electricity to your home and school. It can produce drag that makes satellites drift off their orbits slightly, too.

IS MARS GOING TO CRASH INTO EARTH?

No, Mars isn't on a slow collision course. The planets do a complicated dance around the Sun, with their orbits changing very slightly over patterns of thousands and even millions of years.

HOW LONG DID IT TAKE FOR LIFE TO BEGIN ON EARTH?

It took just 250–500 million years before chemicals got together and made the earliest life forms, but another 3.5 billion years before large life forms started to grow in Earth's oceans. Humans appeared only 200,000 years ago.

IS THERE LIFE ON OTHER PLANETS IN THE SOLAR SYSTEM?

Earth is the only planet to have life. None of the other planets or moons in the solar system are likely to have life, except, just possibly, tiny microbes.

WAS EARTH'S ATMOSPHERE ALWAYS LIKE IT IS NOW?

We breathe the Earth's third attempt at an atmosphere. The first was mostly hydrogen-based gases. Then, lots of volcanoes poured different gases into the atmosphere, so it became mostly nitrogen, carbon dioxide, and water. Finally, tiny bacteria producing oxygen changed the atmosphere again. Now our atmosphere is about a fifth oxygen.

WHAT IS THE MOON MADE OF?

The Earth and the Moon are made of exactly the same materials, so either the Moon is a chunk of the Earth or they both formed from the same stuff.

HOW DID THE MOON FORM?

Our Moon may have formed when something crashed into the Earth 4.5 billion years ago—only about 100 million years after the Earth formed—sending a massive chunk of rock into space, where it stayed orbiting the planet.

IS OUR MOON LARGE COMPARED TO EARTH?

The gas and ice giants have loads of moons, but they never add up to more than 0.1 percent of the mass of their planet. Our Moon, on its own, is 1.2 percent of the mass of Earth. Only the dwarf planet Pluto has a larger moon for its size, at nearly 12 percent of its mass.

ARE THERE SEAS ON THE MOON?

The astronomer Johannes Kepler named the low areas on the Moon "maria" (seas) in the 1600s, thinking there were really areas of land and sea. The maria were actually once flooded with lava that poured from volcanoes. It cooled and hardened to a flat surface. Some maria have been made by asteroids punching holes in the Moon's surface, allowing the lava inside to leak out.

ARE SITES ON THE MOON PROTECTED?

The sites of the Moon landings are "lunar heritage sites," similar to the "world heritage sites" that are protected special places on Earth. The Sea of Tranquility area, with its abandoned Moon junk, will be left as an eternal memorial to our earliest explorations of the Moon.

DID YOU KNOW?

The Moon is extremely dusty. It's entirely covered by a layer of small stones and dust called "regolith." In some of the lowlands, the regolith is just 2 m (6 ft) thick, but on the highlands it can be as deep as 20 m (66 ft).

DID THE MOON HAVE A SISTER?

In 2011, some scientists suggested that Earth once had two moons. The second, smaller, moon would have been 1,270 km (790 miles) across—about one third the size of the surviving Moon.

WHY DID LUNA 2 CRASH ON THE MOON?

The Soviet craft Luna 2 was deliberately crashed into the Moon's surface on September 13, 1959. It was the first object from Earth ever to land on another celestial body. Luna 2 let out a cloud of gas as it neared the Moon that grow to 650 km (400 miles) wide to let scientists on Earth track its progress by telescope. An earlier Luna 1 mission missed the Moon, sailing straight past, and is still moving around the Sun.

WHAT ARE MOON TREES?

Moon trees have grown from spacefaring seeds. Apollo 14 carried 500 tree seeds on a trip around the Moon (but they didn't land). The seeds were from loblolly pine, sycamore, sweetgum, redwood, and douglas fir trees.

HOW DOES LOWER GRAVITY AFFECT ASTRONAUTS?

Lower gravity means astronauts can leap and bounce in ways they never could on Earth. But they also fall over more—we need at least 15 percent of Earth's gravity to give our bodies a good idea of which way is up. Everything else weighs less, too, so astronauts can pick up objects that would be far too heavy for them to lift on Earth.

HOW DOES THE MOON'S ATMOSPHERE COMPARE TO EARTH'S?

If you collected a jug of Earth atmosphere and a jug of thin Moon atmosphere, the Earth jug would contain 10,000 billion times as many molecules (particles) as the Moon jug.

DOES THE MOON HAVE AN ATMOSPHERE?

The Moon's very thin atmosphere is made of helium, argon, possibly neon, ammonia, methane, and carbon dioxide. It's nothing like Earth's atmosphere, which has just 1 percent argon and tiny amounts of the others.

WHAT IS MOONLIGHT?

The surface of the Moon is actually dark, as it doesn't give off any natural light of its own. The bright light we see in the night's sky is light from the Sun reflecting off the surface of the Moon.

HOW LONG DO MOONQUAKES LAST?

Most earthquakes last just a few seconds, and even the longest are over in two minutes. But moonquakes can keep going for ten minutes. If we ever build a space station on the Moon, it will have to be made of slightly flexible material so it isn't cracked by moonquakes.

IS THERE WATER ON THE MOON?

The Moon is bone dry, but only on the surface. Scientists examined tiny glass beads made of volcanic rock on the Moon and found small amounts of water locked into them. The volcanic rock is widespread on the Moon.

Spectacular Space

HOW HOT DOES IT GET ON THE MOON?

Each half of the Moon faces the Sun for half of its long day. It has extreme temperatures, as it has a long time to heat up during the day and cool down at night. It can get as hot as 127 °C (260 °F) during the daytime and drop to -173 °C (-279 °F) at night.

IS THERE ICE ON THE MOON?

There is ice in at least one deep crater at the Moon's south pole. Sunlight never reaches the bottom, and ice can lurk there without thawing for billions of years.

HOW LONG IS A MOON YEAR?

Earth goes around the Sun once in 365 days, which is a year. The Moon's "year" is the 27 days it takes to go around the Earth, which is shorter than its day.

DID YOU KNOW?

There's a dead astronomer on the Moon—or part of one. After the US astronomer Eugene Shoemaker died, some of his ashes were packed on to the Lunar Prospector Lander, which was crashed into the Moon on July 31, 1999.

WILL WE BUILD A MOON BASE?

We might build a base on the Moon. It could be used as a jumping-off point for other space trips, or a research station. A Moon base would need to be well insulated and heated or cooled because of the Moon's extreme hot and cold temperatures. It would have to be completely sealed to keep the air in, and able to recycle air. There is no liquid water, but colonists might be able to extract water that is locked inside rocks or frozen into ice.

WHY DOES THE MOON COME OUT IN THE DAYTIME?

The Moon is above the horizon for roughly 12 hours a day, rising and setting once a day, so it's often visible in the daytime. It often either rises before sunset or sets after sunrise, so it overlaps with daylight and is not always out all night.

IS THERE A PICTURE ON THE MOON?

People have always seen pictures in the patterns on the full Moon, but they haven't all seen the same thing. Some have seen a person with a bundle of sticks, an old man with a lantern, or a woman with a fancy hairstyle and jewels. In China, Japan, and Korea, people see a rabbit making something in a pot—maybe medicine or rice cakes. Other cultures have seen a buffalo, moose, frog, toad, or dragon.

IS THERE ANYTHING GROSS LEFT ON THE MOON?

Some of the stuff left behind is really not very nice—used wet wipes, empty space-food packages, and 96 bags of human waste and vomit!

WHAT HAVE WE LEFT BEHIND ON THE MOON?

For 4.5 billion years, the Moon was a garbage-free zone, then people started going there. Now there's around 187,400 kg (413,100 lb) of clutter there. We've left more than 70 vehicles on the Moon, including crashed spacecraft, used rovers, and discarded modules of spacecraft. Tools including hammers, rakes, shovels, and expensive cameras were all left behind by astronauts.

HOW WAS THE SOLAR SYSTEM FORMED?

The solar system formed around 4.5 billion years ago from a huge, whirling cloud of dust and gas. Pieces of matter started to clump together and, the heavier the lumps got, the more matter they attracted. The biggest lumps eventually became the Sun, the planets, and their moons.

HOW CLOSE IS MERCURY TO THE SUN?

Mercury is about 58 million km (36 million miles) from the Sun, just over a third as far away as Earth.

WHY ARE SOME PLANETS ROCKY AND SOME GASSY?

The solar system has four rocky planets (Mercury, Venus, Earth, and Mars) which are nearest the Sun, and four planets made of gas (Saturn, Jupiter, Uranus and Neptune). When the solar system first formed, it was too hot near the Sun for gases to condense (squeeze together), so they were carried farther out to a colder region. Rock solidifies at much higher temperatures.

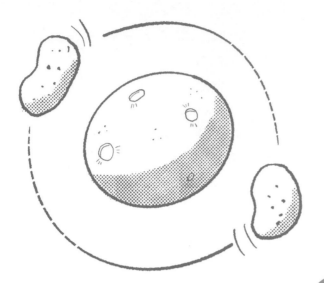

ARE THERE CANALS ON MARS?

In 1877, Italian astronomer Giovanni Schiaparelli drew the first map of Mars. He was convinced he could see straight lines crisscrossing the surface of Mars. He called them "*canali*," which means "channels," but people who didn't speak Italian thought that meant canals. By 1909, astronomers with better telescopes showed there were no canals.

DOES MARS HAVE ANY MOONS?

Mars has two moons, but they're tiny. Phobos is 22.5 km (13.8 miles) across and Demos is just 12.4 km (7.8 miles) across. Both look a little like potatoes—they aren't large enough to have spun themselves into spheres.

WHERE IS THE LARGEST VOLCANO IN THE SOLAR SYSTEM?

Mars has a volcano the size of France. Olympus Mons is 25 km (16 miles) tall, while the highest mountain on Earth, Mount Everest, is just over a third of that size at 8.8 km (5.5 miles) high. Olympus Mons is not only tall—it's about 100 times the volume of the largest volcano on Earth.

HOW MANY MOONS DO JUPITER AND SATURN HAVE?

Saturn has at least 61 and Jupiter at least 79. Because the planets are so large, their gravity reaches far into space, letting them capture passing lumps of rock and ice and dragging them into orbit as moons.

HOW BIG IS THE ASTEROID BELT?

Some of the asteroids are big enough to qualify as dwarf planets themselves. Most of the Asteroid Belt is empty space. If you could stand on one asteroid, you'd struggle to see the next nearest.

WHICH PLANET HAS THE SHORTEST DAY?

The shortest day in the solar system is on Jupiter. There, a day is just under ten hours long, and a year is nearly 12 Earth years long. That means there are more than 10,000 Jupiter days in a Jupiter year.

WHERE IS THE SMELLIEST PLACE IN THE SOLAR SYSTEM?

Jupiter's moon Io is the most volcanic place in the solar system. It has 400 active volcanoes, some of them shooting smelly fumes of sulfur 500 km (310 miles) out into space.

DID YOU KNOW?

On Pluto, you would weigh just one fifteenth of your weight on Earth.

COULD SATURN FLOAT?

Although its rings are rocky, the planet Saturn is light and gassy. It could even float in water—if you could find a bathtub big enough!

WHAT ARE SATURN'S RINGS MADE OF?

Saturn's rings are made of billions of particles of rock, dust, and ice. These might be solid chunks of rock, or perhaps something like dirty snowballs, with smaller lumps frozen together. Some might be the size of a bus, but many are too small to see.

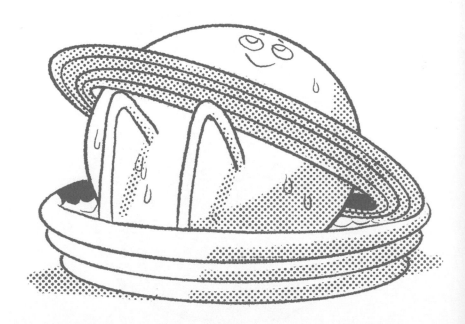

WAS URANUS NEARLY CALLED GEORGE?

Astronomer William Herschel wanted to name Uranus, which he was the first to spot in 1781, after the king of England, so Uranus could have been called George. George was pleased and gave Herschel a lot of money. He used it to build bigger and better telescopes. Herschel became a full-time astronomer who made other important discoveries, but he never found another planet.

WHERE CAN I GO FOR A LONG SUMMER VACATION?

If you lived on Neptune, you might spend your entire life in its 80-year summer— but you could be unlucky and spend your whole life in winter.

WHY ARE NEPTUNE AND URANUS SLUDGY?

Neptune and Uranus are ice planets, but that doesn't mean they're just big chunks of ice. Below the atmosphere is a thick layer of water, methane, and ammonia, which probably form sludgy ice. Right in the middle, there is likely a small core of rock and ice.

IS IT COMPLETELY DARK ON PLUTO?

Pluto is up to 7.5 billion km (4.67 billion miles) away, so it gets a lot less sunlight than Earth. But it's not completely dark—there's as much light at midday on Pluto as there is on Earth just after sunset.

WHERE IS THE SOLAR SYSTEM'S WINDIEST SPOT?

The stormiest storm in the solar system is on Neptune. Its Great Dark Spot, seen in 1979, had winds of 2,400 km/h (1,500 mph). Outside the Spot, winds regularly tear around the planet at nearly 600 m per second (2,000 ft per second).

DOES IT RAIN DIAMONDS ON NEPTUNE?

Storms on Neptune and Uranus might produce diamond "hail" from carbon under huge pressure. The diamond rain could have produced lakes or even oceans of liquid diamond, maybe with floating diamond icebergs.

WHY DO COMETS HAVE TAILS?

If you see a comet in the sky, it looks spectacular—a bright, shining speck with a long glowing tail. But close up, comets are messy lumps of rock and dust. As they get close to the Sun, ice evaporates and the freed gas and dust make up their tail. The tails always face away from the Sun.

IS PLUTO WET?

If you could collect all the water from Earth and make it into a ball, it would be 692 km (430 miles) across. If you did the same to Pluto, it would make a ball 1,368 km (850 miles) across.

COULD THERE BE FISH IN PLUTO'S WATER?

Pluto's huge ocean stretches all around the planet under a thick crust of ice. But it's a poisonous chemical mix that won't be full of Plutonic sea creatures.

WHY WERE PEOPLE FRIGHTENED OF HALLEY'S COMET?

When Halley's comet was due to be seen in 1910, people panicked and thought it would be the end of the world. Scammers even sold comet-proof hats to stop radiation, and pills to protect people from comet "poison."

DID HALLEY'S COMET BRING DISASTER?

In the past, all kinds of disasters were blamed on innocent comets, but they never destroyed the world. But 1910 was the first time scientists could work out that Earth would pass through the comet's tail. People feared it would be poisonous and possibly wipe out life on Earth. But we're all still here ...

WHERE IS THE BEST PLACE TO LOOK FOR LIFE IN SPACE?

Jupiter's moon Europa and Saturn's moon Enceladus are probably the best places to look for life in the solar system beyond Earth. Enceladus has a layer of ice 5 km (3 miles) thick over an ocean 65 km (40 miles) deep. Warm water below the surface could be home to microbes, as it is on Earth.

ARE WE LEAVING THE SUN?

The planets are slowly moving away from the Sun at a rate of about 15 cm (6 in) a year. Scientists aren't sure why. One reason might be that, as the Sun gradually uses itself up making heat and light energy, its mass reduces. It then has less gravitational "pull" to hold on to the planets.

IS THE SUN SLOWING DOWN?

The Sun slows down as it spins, which might reduce its ability to keep the planets nearby. The planets themselves slow it down—their gravitational pull has a braking effect on it. Earth reduces the Sun's speed by three milliseconds each century (0.00003 seconds per year).

WAS THERE REALLY A PLANET NAMED EASTER BUNNY?

There was a dwarf planet named Easter Bunny, but only until it got its permanent name, Makemake. It was given the name because it was found just after Easter in 2005. Makemake was the god of fertility in the myths of the Rapa Nui people of Easter Island.

IS OUR SUN FIT AND HEALTHY?

Our Sun is a common type of star—it's a medium-size, yellow dwarf main sequence star, 4.6 billion years old. That means it's at a healthy stage in the middle of its working life, pumping out energy as heat and light.

WHY IS THE SUN EIGHT MINUTES LATE?

It takes eight minutes for light to reach us from the Sun. Light moves very, very quickly—it covers nearly 400,000 km (248,500 miles) every second. But the Sun is so far away that it still takes eight minutes and 20 seconds for its light to get to us.

HOW HOT IS THE SUN?

The temperature at the Sun's surface is 6,000 °C (11,000 °F). Right in the middle, where all the action is, the temperature is 15 million °C (27 million °F). The atmosphere around the edge of the Sun is called the corona. It's much hotter than the surface, at 1-10 million °C (1.7-17 million °F). No one knows why.

WHAT WILL HAPPEN WHEN THE SUN "DIES?"

When the Sun runs out of hydrogen, it will swell to a red giant, taking in Mercury and Venus. Then it will lose its outer layers, leaving a hard, dense white dwarf about the size of the Earth—but still with much of its mass. Gravity at the surface will be 100,000 times Earth's gravity, and it will be 20 times as hot as the Sun's outer parts are now. Heat escapes slowly into space, so it will take trillions of years to turn into a cold, dead black dwarf.

ARE RED STARS THE HOTTEST?

Red-hot stars are actually the coolest. We're used to thinking of red things as super hot, but that's only because we link fire and heat with red. Red is the first type of light to shine out as something gets hot, so it comes from the coolest hot things. The hottest stars shine with pale blue light.

IS OUR SUN QUITE A SMALL STAR?

Nearly every star you can see is bigger than the Sun. Stars come in lots of sizes, but they're a long way away. From Earth, you can only see the biggest and brightest stars. The Sun is the fourth smallest star we can see from Earth without a telescope or binoculars. The other three are very faint.

IS THE POLE STAR BRIGHTER THAN OUR SUN?

The Pole Star, Polaris, is a bright star in the night sky. It's 2,200 times as bright as the Sun, but so far away it looks like a pinprick.

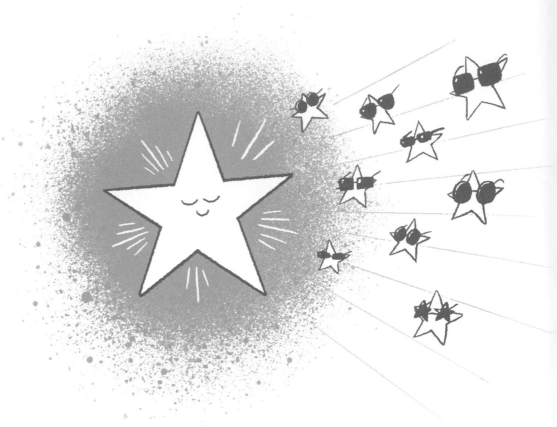

WHERE IS THE NEXT-NEAREST STAR?

After the Sun, the next-nearest star is called Proxima Centauri. It's nearly 40 trillion km (25 trillion miles) away.

WHICH STAR IS THE BRIGHTEST?

The brightest star is called Pistol. It shines up to 10 million times as brightly as the Sun. So much radiation comes from it that even if it has any planets they could not support life.

HOW LONG WOULD IT TAKE TO GET TO PROXIMA CENTAURI?

Even in the fastest spacecraft we have, it would take 76,000 years to get Proxima Centauri.

WHERE IS THE MILKY WAY IN SPACE?

The Milky Way is part of a group of galaxies called, unimaginatively, the Local Group. Between one billion and one trillion years from now, the Milky Way and all the other galaxies of the Local Group will have merged into a single mega galaxy.

ARE ALL THE STARS IN THE SKY IN OUR GALAXY?

All the stars you can see at night are in our galaxy, the Milky Way. The Milky Way is so vast, and the stars in it so bright, that we can't see the stars outside it.

HOW BIG ARE SUNSPOTS?

They're not small spots—they can be 160,000 km (100,000 miles) across. That's 12 times as wide as the Earth.

WHAT IS A SUPERNOVA?

Stars more than eight times the mass of the Sun eventually explode in a spectacular supernova. The explosion lasts a week or more, shining more brightly than any star in the sky. The last supernova seen clearly from Earth happened in 1604.

WHAT IS A BLACK HOLE?

A black hole isn't a hole at all. It's an area where matter is so squashed there is no space in it at all, not even within the atoms. Anything that gets too close to a black hole is pulled toward it and squashed along with everything else. That's how black holes grow.

WHAT'S IN THE MIDDLE OF THE MILKY WAY?

There is probably a supermassive black hole at the middle of the Milky Way. It has the mass of 4 million Suns and is called Sagittarius A* (pronounced "A-star"). All galaxies probably have a huge black hole in the middle, with the mass of millions or billions of stars crushed into a small space. As they take in more dust, gas, and other matter, they grow even larger.

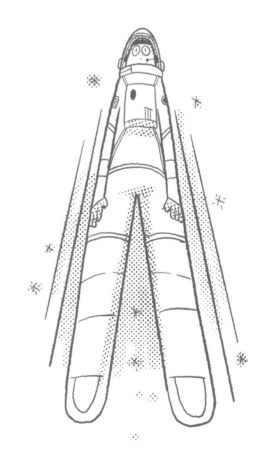

WHAT HAPPENS IF YOU GET SUCKED INTO A BLACK HOLE?

Most astronomers think matter that gets pulled into a black hole is compressed and destroyed. But a few think black holes are tunnels to another universe. At the end of the tunnel—or wormhole—the matter is spat out of a white hole where it's used to make ... well, whatever that universe has in it.